AGILE METHODOLOGY

A Beginner's Guide to Agile Method and Principles

WESLEY CLARK

Table of Contents

Introduction

An often confusing and occasionally controversial subject in both software development and project management, is "What is Agile?" The Beginner's Guide to Agile Method and Principles covers what Agile is and explains what it is not. Readers will learn to quickly identify false claims of "Agile" products while also learning how to implement Agile methods in their own work.

Day to day development and project management practices make for an environment of continued growth, and that is exactly what someone new to Agile needs. Come into this book with an open mind, and explore what opportunities await you in project management and software development. Not only can understanding more about Agile give you an edge in job market competition, but it can help you change how you work. Through Agile principles, you can navigate teamwork, leadership, and expectations with more precision and understanding. Implement the Agile principles into more than just software development to change how you impact your workplace and your company's customers.

Chapter One

Defining Project Management and Agile Method

What is Agile methodology, and where does it fit into most businesses operations? To answer simply, Agile is a system of values and principles, which lend themselves to specific niches of project management. However, that rather simple explanation can't begin to encompass everything that agile methods do. It also doesn't begin to touch on the nuances of the Agile principles, or how Agile fits into project management. To develop a foundation for understanding Agile methodology, you'll need to have a basic grasp on project management.

Project management is the practice of planning, acting upon that plan, and controlling your team in such a way that it accomplishes the specific goals. Now, that applies to most people in the workforce. Specific project managers, or professional project managers such as Six Sigma certified project leaders, usually put their focus on accomplishing big goals. Agile, in project management, usually refers to the development or creation of a software or program. So, taking the focus on Agile into consideration, you are most likely to use Agile methods and the guiding principles through project management on a software creation team. The two have a lot of common ground in terms of fundamental working aspects. For example, project management requires the soft skill of understanding when to pivot and respond to unexpected change. Then, in Agile, one of the foundational principles essentially says to respond to change without hesitation. The overlap between project management expectations and Agile methods is intentional. You'll see through exploring the brief history of Agile and these well-founded principles that the project management and Agile run hand-in-hand at nearly every turn.

There might be some concern that you or your team has a lack of experience in project management. However, as mentioned before, nearly everyone has some experience in project management through either leadership or teamwork. Even as early as middle or secondary school level students must work together in team projects to complete a single goal. Typically, these groups will either have a leader, or each person will perform a specific task or function. These practices and assignments help nearly every student build soft and hard skills that apply to project management. Even with only very basic knowledge of teamwork, you can begin to explore and understand Agile methods in action through project management.

When looking at the leadership position, project management does require that the person creating the project, understand a few key aspects. A project manager should be able to set the scope of the work and determine a time frame. Often in school projects, the teacher acts as the "leader." A project management leader should also clear layout expectations for the quality of the work and explain to the team how that quality is vital to reach the goal. When working with project management through a business perspective and specifically within Agile expectations, the leader must work with the restrictions of a set budget.

Additionally, they may run into scarce resources or resources, which are in generally, short supply. Agile projects are notorious for lacking in people resources, and it's partially because leaders want to have more control over quality. No less than three of the twelve Agile principles address the balance between resources, quality, and using both wisely.

Standard skills expected of project managers and those working on Agile projects include a mix of both hard and soft skills. Or in other words, skills that associate with taught lessons, certifications, or some extent of experience and skills, which come from intrapersonal abilities.

Hard skills for project managers and Agile developers include cost control, risk management, contract management, and business writing. There are many instances where an Agile project leader or manager may have a few but not all of these skills. If you are just getting into project management or looking to cultivate your skills through Agile projects, then you will learn many of these skills while you gain experience. Agile projects often require their leaders to audit the project to ensure that the team is on track to hit not only deadlines but quality expectations as well. Then they must often write case reviews, white papers, or case studies explaining the Agile software that the team developed. Just keep in mind that you don't have to be the best writer, or the best auditor, or even the best at risk management. However, you do need to excel in various soft skills to make up for any gaps in your hard skills.

Soft skills for Agile project leaders boil down to three primary abilities. Agile project leaders need the ability to lead a team, to communicate effectively, and to delegate tasks appropriately. Although these seem like three very straightforward expectations, executing these skills consistently without diminishing the quality of the project is nothing short of outstanding. Many of these skills play a role in Agile values and team constructs. Because Agile projects and methods rely on teamwork, it is these soft skills that are often less negotiable. Many employers are willing to allow new project managers to develop through experience. However, if an employee is known for their ineffective communication or poor delegating abilities, it is less likely that they will be brought onto Agile projects.

Additional soft skills that can play a massive role in working on Agile projects include the ability to negotiate, think critically, and work with a high level of organization. These skills can help you make up for a lack of communication or leadership abilities. It's more likely that they will land you a spot on the team, and less of a leadership role. Self-organization is critical as you're working with numerous moving parts and different people who are bringing in various information and skills. With well-developed organizational skills, you can work through the chaos that often has some presence in Agile projects.

An important note in explaining the foundation of Agile methods and project management is that Agile principles address two key areas of project management. First, Agile methodology helps ensure that the end-result delivers high value for both the end-user and the stakeholders. Second, Agile methods ensure that the project adapts for internal and external factors which change as the project progresses. This particular area of Agile requires much more explanation. Unfortunately, these two foundational aspects of Agile methods cause quite a bit of confusion.

Many people see Agile as separate from project management, as a standalone certification similar to LEAN or Six Sigma. Agile is neither of those things, as explained, Agile fits in with project management in specific areas. Successful Agile software development relies on excellent project management and exceptional understanding and execution of Agile principles and values. Another common source of confusion regarding Agile is that companies and software claim to be "Agile," which is not the proper application of the term. A company can create software through Agile methods. A company can even use the Agile principles to guide their decision making and day-to-day operations. However, using "Agile" to describe a company or software is inaccurate.

Agile simply cannot apply to every single project or aspect of business operations. But because so many of the Agile principles and values come into play in the core of project management is makes it difficult to separate the definitions clearly. In the most succinct terms, Agile is a framework of values, principles, and tools or methods. They are ever-present in the development of certain types of software and are often applicable in various other projects as well. With this in mind, it's clear to see the more common misconceptions regarding Agile methods such as companies claiming to offer Agile services, or Agile software. Keep these specifics about Agile claims in mind as you read through and learn more about Agile and applying the core principles.

One of the most prominent descriptors or labels associated with Agile is the ability to adapt and respond to change. Responsiveness is a significant aspect of Agile principles. The many Agile methods are built with safety nets to accommodate substantial change while not losing the charter or course set for the completion of the project. Agile will always fall back to the core principles and values. However, the practices, methods, tools, and frameworks can change, flex, and otherwise bend to fit the project's needs. Throughout this book, you can see how the umbrella term of Agile comes into play in various Agile methods. You'll also have the chance to explore how the different techniques contribute to the Agile team dynamic and why this team setup is so unique. The entirety of the philosophy, system, and the many methodologies contained within Agile make it advantageous for anyone working in close proximity to software development.

Chapter Two

History of Agile Methodology

B etween the 1940s and 1970, there was little available in terms of software for small business or home use. However, a lot of that changed in 1970 when computers became more readily available. Early in the 1970s, various big companies around the world took their first steps towards technological transformation. All the while, people at home were bringing in these devices as well. Up until that point the only people who really needed to concern themselves with coding, or programming in its earliest forms were working within the government on projects such as the Apollo Mission. But what does all this have to do with Agile?

In the early 1970s, people began purchasing computers for home, and business use and that same era marks the birth of the Unix operating system. Having a base operating system for computers meant that programmers, developers, and coders could create packaged software for numerous users. The Unix operating system still exists today with the most famous rendition being macOS used on Macintosh or Apple devices. Others may be even more familiar with Linux, a close relative of Unix. The seventies had a boom of software and computer hardware advancements.

Notably, SAP became the first enterprise software creation company and delivered software solutions for business operations. Microsoft emerged in 1975, creating software explicitly for "micro-computers," and in 1976, Apple released the first personal computer. In the following decades, both hardware and software would continue to evolve, adapt, and expand the use of software globally. It was this first wave of adaptive software development, which sparked what would eventually be known as Agile. Not to mention that they were beginning to perfect the iterative as well as incremental development methodologies used in software development. There are a few methodologies, which break into that incremental and iterative structure.

Then the 1990s gave birth to many tools that would eventually be known to fit within the Agile repertoire. Rapid application development, DSDM, Scrum, Crystal Clear, and extreme programming came between the years 1991 and 1997. Even though these methods predate the original Agile Manifesto, it's clear that the fundamental practices, methods, and tools used here all associate to Agile. Now they are now known as Agile development techniques. These tools also stood apart and were used by different thought leaders. In fact, the gap between delivering software and the advancement of business technology throughout the 1990s was called the application development crisis. The difference between a business need and software delivery was about three years. Part of this lag was due to the confines of developers and development teams. Yes, businesses were moving faster than anyone ever thought possible. However, the bigger problem was the apparent battle between expectations and the ability to work in a way, which would allow developers to reach those expectations. Most developers were not put in charge of their projects.

In fact, most companies would rely on sole thought leaders to only step in after much of the work was done. That resulted in projects going from square one to completion many times over.

This brief history of software, which leads up to, the creation of the Agile manifesto is extraordinarily essential. All of the developers who took part in crafting the manifesto had varying years of experience. Some had been working professionally at the time of the first personal computer while others took part in founding extreme programming or scrum. Looking back, it's clear that the minds, which founded Agile, had played a significant role in sculpting the landscape around software development. Without knowing it, the founders of Agile had been working towards creating greater principles for successful software development projects and project management for decades.

Then in 2001, after the dotcom bust, and y2K the founding group of Agile software developers came together. The seventeen founders and signatories on the Agile Manifesto include: Dave Thomas, Brian Marick, Martin Fowler, Ward Cunningham, Jon Kern, Jeff Sutherland, Ken Schwaber, Ron Jeffries, Alistair Cockburn, Arie van Bennekum, Andrew Hunt, Steve Mellor, Jim Highsmith, Mike Beedle, Kent Beck, James Grenning, and Robert C. Martin.

In February of 2001, these software development professionals and leaders met together in Utah at the Snowbird Ski Resort nestled within the Wasatch mountains. When meeting, each person attending knew that they would have like minds surrounding them and others who had led heavyweight-programming methods. They also knew that the goal of their meeting was to find a different way to go about the software development process. Before this meeting, each person was known as a rebel of sorts by bending the rules, working in unorthodox manners, and otherwise, exploring the uncertain areas of software development. The problem was that they alone were trying to break the mold of working within the confines of a manufacturing mindset. Often the companies they worked for wanted to see software developed the same way you might run a manufacturing process. These leaders understood that the software development process much more closely resembled new-product development and engineering approaches. An excellent quote from NASA's Robert Frost helps explain the difference between development and manufacturing. *"... Why does it take six years to develop a new airplane when it shares 90% of its 'DNA' with the previous model? The answer is that they are complex devices... there is little tolerance for imprecision and error.* "Although software development alone does not put people on the moon, the sentiment is the same. It is one thing to build a system that will work again and again for years to come. It is quite another thing to develop and create something new, no matter how much it resembles an older system. The thought leaders that met and would form Agile understood that mindset because they had seen and worked with that obstacle for decades. They had experienced success and failure using a wide variety of tools and frameworks. Those tools and frameworks never guaranteed success on any given project. However, most of the companies relying on them did not understand this; they had implemented LEAN and other methodologies into every aspect of their operations. Essentially companies employing software developers prior to the Agile Manifesto wanted their development teams to work with the same efficiency and autonomy of manufacturing teams. Aside from the manufacturing mindset struggle, there was another issue that nearly every software developer experienced through the 1990s and early 2000s. The documentation requirements were arduous and nearly debilitating. The software design processes weren't succinct, and the term "heavy-weight" was the only way to describe the sheer volume of work that each project required. When this team met up, they ended up naming themselves, "The Agile Alliance" and they created a manifesto of twelve principles and four values. Overall their goals were to create deep-set themes that would fuel development, rather than a strict outline of tools. They knew that "plug-and-play" tools or methods that were existent in Six Sigma and LEAN philosophies would work here. The idea of "use (tool) for (problem) to achieve (result)" doesn't work primarily because of the substantial changes that software developers face in every single project. The crisis through the 1990s with the three-year delay in development came because the developers weren't able to pivot or adapt to changes. The Agile manifesto addressed these big-picture issues rather than assigning tools to certain obstacles. In fact, much of the Agile Manifesto looks at the human element of creation and project management.

To get to the core of things, Agile is not about working away from methodologies. Often called the Agile method, and having the many tools called Agile methodologies shows that the creation of this manifesto was not about eliminating tools, frameworks, or structures. They did aim to free themselves from the requirements of unnecessary steps, documentation, or methodologies, which didn't fit the bill for the project. Software developers, including those involved in founding the Agile Alliance, reported making accurate estimates in regard to time for projects or expected necessary resources. However, many of their plans went awry when the manager in charge of the project was unable to provide resources or took manpower away from the project. Kent Beck of the Agile Alliance posted his recollection of a job he worked on during the 1990s. He was well established and estimated that the software development would require six weeks with a two people team. However, very early into the project, the manager pulled the second person, Beck's teammate, off the project. The entire project took Beck twelve weeks to complete, and for much of that time, Beck felt as if he were failing and the manager overseeing the project informed him that he was failing. It was only much later that he realized that his time estimates were very accurate and that his manager was unable to provide the necessary resources. These were the instances that developers saw in all variety of industries. It was these issued that led them to come together and create the Agile Alliance.

After the publication of the Agile values and principles, the Agile movement took off. It worked to restore the good name of software developers and to embrace useful documentation and useful methodologies. The movement continues to prosper with new developers and project managers embarking on studying Agile in an effort to become better managers and better teammates.

While the meeting, which led to the Agile Alliance formation, is well-known, much of the Agile movement is not. Notorious for avoiding documentation whenever possible it seems that the movement itself has escaped formal record. The rather brief history of Agile, however, does give a substantial amount of insight into the events, which prompted this monumental meeting of minds. It also helps to clear up confusion about why the Agile principles or methods are so people-centric when the application of the methodologies is for software development. There is little more to learn about the Agile Alliance, although nearly all of them went on to become published authors. They almost all speak at great length, or work as consultants on their respective forte or to help companies implement Agile principles within their software development teams. Some companies have attempted to impart their Agile principles into their greater business operations. A few of the Agile Alliance have facilitated these efforts, although very few companies seem to stick with it after a few years. Ultimately, the greater public may not see much more from this particular group. Instead, it is more likely that a new collection of leading software development minds will take up the Agile mantle when another crisis strikes the industry.

Chapter Three

Understanding the Agile Manifesto

The manifesto and principles are technically two separate documents and to understand the principles you must have a deep understanding of the manifesto. Through the history of Agile, you learned about what environmental conditions brought these great minds together. Their work history and experience played a massive role in why this manifesto reads more about people and soft skills than the development of software.

The manifesto is short and leaves little room for misinterpretation. Together the seventeen men of the Agile Alliance knew that they could not craft some long and drawn out document. To be taken seriously, they needed to get right to the point and figure out how to create a common ground that every software developer could agree upon.

The introduction of the manifesto reads through with an in real-time goal. The manifesto says, *"We are uncovering better ways of developing software by doing it and helping others do it."* That line speaks very clearly. It says that the only way that software development improves is through the act of continuing to develop software. It's also a declaration as if the Agile Alliance were announcing, "Hey! We're good at our jobs, and we're going to help others be great at their jobs!"

Without a doubt, that introductory phrase helped build the steam that continues to propel the Agile movement forward even today. We're closely approaching the twentieth anniversary of the Agile meeting, and even now that line is correct, direct and applicable for the leaders of software development currently.

The manifesto then lists the four primary values which fuel agile processes, methodology, and teams. More on these values later. In this chapter, we're looking exclusively at the declarations and the underlying meaning. As mentioned above the introductory clause was succinct and delivered a no-nonsense stance before they discussed their values. One of the biggest motivators for this type of introduction was that the team knew their values didn't focus on software. Instead, they focused on the human element behind software development. Mostly if they didn't come out of the gate swinging, no one would take them seriously. There was an across the board concern that they would not be taken seriously with their manifesto and goal because they were taking something cold and critical such as software development and looking at the warmer side. They even incorporated and addressed this concern in the format of their manifesto.

When looking at the Agile Manifesto, it's clear that nothing goes unnoticed by a software developer. Every detail here, including the wording, structure, and deliverance of the message was thoroughly thought through. Visually the manifesto looks more like a poem, or even a list rather than what people typically expect from a manifesto. When introducing the values, they purposefully placed higher priority items on the right and lesser priority items on the left. They did this to address many misconceptions about the expectations and needs of software developers.

Without getting into much detail about the values themselves, you can see the stark comparison between the respective right and left side of things quickly. The first value in the list of four reads, *"Individuals and interactions over processes and tools. "*The rest of the list continues to read through as intangible v. tangible, or immeasurable v. measurable. With this format, the Agile Alliance was able to say; we understand that this is what businesses expect of software developers. They were also able to say, but these are the things we need to make software development projects a success. They declared that they weren't automatons. They weren't capable of pumping out successful software solution after a successful software solution if they were forced to work alone and under duress.

The closing statement of the manifesto is simply, *"That is, while there is value in the items on the right, we value the items on the left more."* Again, this is repeating the sentiment that yes, things such as processes and documentation are important. But they are not as important as change responsiveness or collaboration. Ultimately, this wording and this layout became a rallying cry for many within software development and the tech field. Not only were people advocating for greater focus on the dull side of development, but they were advocating for long-term plans towards changing focus. This closing left no room for discussion. It wasn't an initiation to talk about how the development community was feeling or why these thought leaders felt the need to come together and set the record straight. It left with a final summation of the values and explained their viewpoint.

When considering where these thought leaders were at, it's almost a nod any one of history's great revolutions. A group of development leaders came together and decided that there was to be no more nonsense. These software developers had made substantial advancements in their industry. They learned countless coding languages as the environment around them changed, and still, there was no guarantee of success on any project. The only guarantees were that each project would be stressful, have too few resources, have little to no structure from people who understood the project, and eventually would reach completion. There were no tools or methodologies, or processes, which were formal enough to implement across the board. Because of the nature of rapid change in the tech industry, that's still hard to come by, and the tools from Agile only stand because they are subject to change.

What is the big picture of this very small manifesto? This group needed to speak to one type of person in the entire business world. They needed to reach the Chief Executives of any business, which was interested in developing software for any purpose. Even before laying out the principles, they put it down that these were the inarguable rules of working with the Agile Alliance. They would no longer put up with excessive documentation requirements or use tools that didn't fit into the project. They also, made a promise here, although it often goes unnoticed. Essentially throughout the manifesto, the Agile group declared that they could do exactly what they were supposed to do, develop software if their conditions were met. They were telling chief executives that they could create working software that provided value to the customer. But only if they were allowed to work in a manner that would enable them to succeed. This manifesto was written by people who had encountered many contracts and experienced both success and failure. Together this group knew what worked and what didn't. They just needed to format it in such a way that others would see it, understand it, and acknowledge that they were right. To say the least, they succeeded. After 2001 the industries outlook and work environment for software developers changed drastically. Even now, the industry continues to change, and Agile is still evolving. In recent years there have been concerns about the Agile-Industrial Complex. Aside from concerns about the industrial impact on Agile's values, other advancements include the building of more trusting teams. This largely comes from developers learning Agile values before they enter the workforce. Now, Agile is largely engrained within the software development community.

Chapter Four

Principles Which Define and
Shape Project Management – Part 1

The principles of the Agile Alliance stand to guide the development of software and apply through all associated Agile methodologies. It is these principles, which have fueled the implementation of the Agile thought processes into aspects of work outside of software development. It's true that many of these principles can be applied to people management, business process development, and even departments such as compliance. These principles don't leave much room independently for misinterpretation. However, together, there is more than enough room for confusion.

Looking at these principles calls on using two abilities. First, you must be able to see the big pictures. Often referred to as 'seeing the forest, not the trees,' big picture thinkers can give these principles a context. That context is software development, and the people who miss out on the big picture will often try to apply these principles in ways that have little to no effect. You'll see throughout that each principle may show some resemblance or a nod to business management principles or tactics. The reason for their restatement here is to clarify the idea through the lens of a software development team. Anyone familiar with Six Sigma, LEAN or other process management techniques will identify much of the language used here.

The second ability that you need to employ when reading through these principles is the capacity to set an endpoint. Many companies have claimed that they 'do agile' in every department or that they use Agile techniques every day. These are leaders who read the principles and did not know where to stop. The goal of the principles is to guide a team, not a company. Additionally, those who attempt to put their energy into up scaling these principles will miss out on their core value. Here we will deep dive into each principle and have a look at the big picture, the details, and where the application of the principle should end.

Now, on large scale teams or for companies that only produce software, it is possible to apply these principles daily. Keep in mind that it is because they are developing software daily. Their development teams are meeting daily, and the people involved have had some say in how they want to work.

Principle One

> *"Our highest priority is to satisfy the customer through early and continuous delivery of valuable software."*

The most direct and 'big picture' scope of this principle is that software developers will focus on delivering consistently valuable software, frequently, to provide customer satisfaction. Now, knowing a bit about what brought the Agile Alliance together, it's clear that this phrasing and directness was very purposeful. At face-value, everything about the statement is true and easy to apply. There are a few deeper undertones; however, this is no hidden meaning here.

For those familiar with the techniques of Six Sigma process management, then you may have caught onto a keyword here already. That keyword of "customer" can mean their manager, the end-user, or a different department within the company. Because they're creating software rather than a product that would surely go through standard retail value chains, there are a wide variety of customers involved. For example, when developing software, it's possible that the development team must meet the expectations of their manager, while also ensuring that the software will benefit the end-user. In that turn, if their company sells the software to another company for distribution, that purchasing company is also a customer.

Then there is the presence of another critical statement, "… early and continuous delivery of valuable software." Choosing the end, the first principle this way set the foundation for something that will ring throughout the remaining principles. The Agile Alliance focused on principles for delivering valuable software, not simply software that will sell or function on a fundamental level. They wanted to ensure that their software gave something to the company, as well as the end-user. They also gave their first reference to a timeline. Because of the significant and constant changes within the tech industry, software developers know that the sooner they complete a project, the less likely that they'll make excessive changes during development. By leaving the statement on the time frame as "early and continuous," it opens the door between the developing team and the managers or employers to discuss a time frame between them. There was no promise here, such as completing software within so many weeks or delivering within so many days of a deadline. The open nature of the phrase "early and continuous" satisfies a reference for time. While the wording also acknowledges that software needs updating. A developers' job is not done simply because the software is in use by the end-user.

So where is the line drawn here? It's clear that the line for the first principle is regarding software development. This principle does not transpose or translate to other department or job functions well, and it's best not to try to make it work.

Principle Two

> *"Welcome changing requirements, even late in development. Agile processes harness change for the customer's competitive advantage."*

Again, here is another straightforward principle, which the Agile Alliance wanted all software developers to implement into their practices. The idea of welcoming change breaks some of the ice when it comes to an understanding of your work environment. But it also helps to open some of the communication between the business end and the developers on the team. Throughout the 1990s that a substantial gap of three years between the software need and the delivery was primarily due to issues with changes. Either a company would not request necessary changes until a determined point in the development process, or sometimes they would request changes at all. To the companies involved, changes weren't part of the plan, and what it resulted in was a lot of software was out of date on the day of its release. Then the team would have to scramble to put together updates, create change logs, and more. On a different note, some projects were delayed heavily because of constant changes and the development team's resistance to change. It is disheartening to work on a project and then be told to redo something or change the core of something that

23

will be the onset of much more work. It is disheartening for the people on that team to realize that their progress has just been set back by days, weeks, or even months.

So, where should people draw the line with these principles? When does it stop applying? This principle does apply across all software development teams, and in many cases, the general sentiment should apply to many other areas of work. However, there are restrictions on the capacity of this principle. First, it seems like any change is welcome, but when you evaluate the phrasing, there are qualifiers for welcoming change. They welcome changing "requirement" and take into consideration the customer's advantage. Mostly, they're not willing to accept change for the sake of it, but if the customers need something new, then that change is welcome. The second qualifier is just that the customer's need. This principle would not apply to a change that came about because someone on the team liked a specific idea. It would not even apply when a manager requested a change without some explanation about how that change would impact the customer.

The second principle is proof of the overall intention of the manifesto and the Agile Alliance. It stands that the most critical aspects of software development are delivering valuable, functioning software early and fast.

You can see this principle in constant use through scrum methodologies. A scrum team will enhance competitiveness and give a clear advantage because of this principle.

Principle Three

"Deliver working software frequently, from a couple of weeks to a couple of months with a preference to the shorter timescale."

Okay, the precise terms and takeaways here include, "working software," "frequently," and "shorter timescale." One of the major points that are driven home in this principle is that the software must be working. The Agile Alliance knew that deliverance of not functioning software would harm the industry as a whole. It would give all software developers a poor reputation. And it could have put a damper on the tech advances we've seen in the last two decades. If teams, before the Agile Manifesto publication, were pushing out software which functioned inadequately or blatantly didn't work that would have become the norm. This principle broke the expectation of software development. It stood as the developers proclaiming that they wanted to deliver working software and that they wanted to do it quickly.

Thankfully, when it comes to restricting this principle, there is little room to apply it outside of software development. However, there are some aspects of this principle, which people have dug into and pulled out something else.

First, this principle made people begin to question the definition of done. Prior to the Agile Alliance, many software developers completed the project as they were told to. However, it's difficult for anyone outside of programming to understand what completion means and returning to a project, again and again, is a waste of time. Having a clear definition of done comes from the statement of delivering working software frequently. Then the attachment of a timeframe made it possible for developers to say, this is the goal.

Second, the condition of satisfaction became a concern born out of this principle. It's unclear why because many other principles speak more on satisfaction. This principle is one of the shining examples of how business professionals have tried to make Agile something closer to LEAN.

Finally, the aspect of waste management is present here. However, again, it doesn't mean that this principle guides business decisions. It guides a team, and the structure of these principles relies on a timetable. The declaration here is that the ideal completion of any software development project is within a few weeks or months.

Ultimately, this principle is taken out of context often, and it's likely because it's such an important principle to Agile. It's a promise of delivery and functionality, which is something that few other creative professionals can guarantee on a large scale.

Principle Four

"Businesspeople and developers must work together daily throughout the project."

Right out of the gate, this principle addresses a big elephant in the room. There are business people, and there are software developers, and neither fully understands the duties of the other. The administrative staff doesn't usually know the nuances of development, and developers have trouble seeing the gaps between management and external expectations. Yes, there is a divide, but this principle continues to say that it is absolutely critical that both work together daily. There cannot be weekly, or end of the month check-ins. There needs to be daily contact for these projects to stay one time and reach completion with some level of efficiency.

As a result of this principle, Agile developed several terms of the people involved. The business people involved in software development programs are often called the 'Product Owner,' a term that is close to the terminology of Six Sigma, where they refer to the external manager involved as the Process Owner. The people who brought together the principles and values of Agile were very familiar with project management, and they understood that human involvement is the cornerstone of a successful project. No matter the subject or goals, the people involved must work together daily.

This principle is one that really can stretch across so many industries and job functions. You can, in essence, replace "developers" with nearly anything. You can say, "Businesspeople and nurses must work together daily..." and it would be true. This principle is perhaps the only one that would benefit from a restrictive acknowledgment. Not only can the people involved cultivate positive relationships, but they can focus on building long-term relationships as well.

The ultimate takeaway from this principle is that Agile exists to invoke certain behaviors. Of those behaviors are commitment, communication, and collaboration. Something that many of us could benefit from if we worked at it.

Chapter Five

Principles Which Define
and Shape Project Management – Part 2

The principles continue to build upon the elements of daily duties and overarching goals for software developers. All of these principles dive into what it means for both software developers and the Product Owners that they collaborate with on these projects.

Principle Five

> *"Build projects around motivated individuals. Give them the environment and support they need and trust them to get the job done."*

We have something new with this principle, and it begins to set expectations for the developers. The prior principles looked at the essence of the project, the goals, and the behaviors of all involved. Now, principle five essentially says, if you're not motivated, then get out. The Agile Alliance once again takes control and shows the rest of the world with this principle that they know some people don't pull their weight.

Then they follow that up with a request. Give motivated individuals an environment that will continue to produce motivation. Much like a self-perpetuation machine, motivation doesn't run out when you have support around you. People feel burned out and lose motivation because they feel as if they're dealing with managers who don't trust them. Environments, which cut down autonomy and are filled with strife don't have motivated individuals.

The big picture of this principle is that when organizing a project, the Product Owner should give consideration as to the type of personality that they hire. Addressing concerns about whether that person will take responsibility for their role in the project early can help lead the team to success. Then there is the second line of this principle, providing an environment of support and trust. Here is where the Agile Alliance begins to try to get the buy-in of lesser-controlled environments. Agile projects rely on the buy-in of management and executives. They need the flex and support of higher up professionals so they can create an environment that they work well in.

This principle has had a vast amount of application through the years, and while some companies excel with it, others don't. Essentially, this principle tells managers to stop micromanaging and to let go control over some, if not all, aspects of a project. Reasonably, many managers have trouble handling this advice. However, it hasn't stopped companies from trying to force management into these positions from the top-down.

Understanding a buy-in goes beyond project management, and many in executive positions come across the concept daily. A buy-in is getting the person who has control, or some say over a sector of work to choose to do what you want them to do. Dale Carnegie explained it fluently in *How to Win Friends and Influence People;* he stated that there is only one single way to get anyone to do anything at all. You must make them want to do it. This principle is stated in a very direct manner, and more than a few managers have read this line and scoffed. The thought that they didn't have to give anyone support or trust no doubt ran through their mind. But that says something more about that particular leader. Anyone who rejects the idea that a working relationship needs trust and support is not familiar with working with people, and probably shouldn't be in a management position. No doubt people who respond in such a way to this principle will lead to many more project failures than project successes.

Principle Six

> *"The most efficient and effective method of conveying information to and within a development team is a face-to-face conversation."*

Who hasn't experienced this frustrating incident when at work, on a team, or even in school? Although the Agile Alliance wrote out their manifesto years before the first iPhone, they knew what direction the world was heading towards. The less time spent communicating face-to-face, the more opportunity there is for miscommunication. You've probably read a text or email in an angry voice, while the person who wrote it was simply in a hurry or used auto fill and didn't mean to sound callous or upset at all.

Face-to-face communication allows both people and all people involved to not only receive information but to perceive body language as well. Most of the time, we rely on body language, and it can make a difference. Image a motivational, "Let's get this done," with a smile and a huddle-breaking clap. Then compare that feeling to an email that simply reads, "Let's get this done." One is cold, and the other gives you a boost. These miscommunications happen all the time, and it changes how people feel about their work. One of the methodologies that will appear later is SCRUM, and it should happen for teams daily. This tool is the reason that many leaders from restaurant managers to executives hold daily meetings or huddles. The goal is to meet up about the team's goals and work status, then review that progress, and the following day repeat. That is a very condensed explanation of the framework. But, the standing rule on SCRUM meetings is that they must be in person. They cannot happen through email, chat, text, or phone. For remote workers some schedule Video chat times so everyone in the team can see the people they're speaking with during the meeting.

This principle can apply throughout all industries. Yes, or probably. Many industries now don't work with teams, and in fact, the gig economy has made many people solopreneurs or independent contractors that never interact with their working peers. Instead, they primary access customers and in that there is no need for this type of communication. Ultimately, it's best to keep this principle scaled down to a team-by-team basis. Your whole company doesn't need to meet regularly at all unless your company is one succinct team of a few people. However, the concept behind this principle is something that any working person can value. You can make it something that you personally value and strive to make face-to-face communications the preference whenever possible. Don't be afraid to apply this principle in other ways outside of software development but do be wary about forcing others to adopt this practice.

Principle Seven

"Working software is the primary measure of progress."

One struggle that many people in product creation as well as software development experience is unnecessary metrics. While sales teams often resort to KPIs to measure their success, and companies rely on QA to see progress, those don't work here. Software development is a process of creation, and that means that any unnecessary metric to gauge profess will just slow down the progress. This principle stands to show that teams must know whether they're going in the right direction or not just based on how well the software works.

The big picture here? Does it work? If it doesn't work, then you're not far enough along in the project yet. When it begins to work, you can begin to tool and tailor other aspects, but the question will always return to, does the software work?

Are there other areas where this principle can apply? Across the board, probably not. This principle is very specific software creation. Imagine using this principle when creating a painting, writing a book, or opening a business. Would it work? No. Using this principle wouldn't work in those situations because oftentimes, working isn't the bare minimum. For example, opening a business, you might ask yourself, does a cash register work in its most basic form? Yes. Essentially you could have a lockbox and a calculator and call it a cash register. But, will that system give you any help when it comes to assessing what you owe in sales tax? No. These grand processes, which take place on a massive scale, need each aspect of operations to lend itself to another element of a business. However, when you zoom in on software development, you can apply this very raw and direct principle.

There's also the special aspect of this very short phrase. Working software is only a measure of progress. It's not a measure of completion. Asking "does the software work?" at daily SCRUM meetings can tell Product Owners were the project stands, and if the team needs help.

Principle Eight

"Agile processes promote sustainable development. The sponsors, developers, and users should be able to maintain a constant pace indefinitely."

Here is the first mention of agile processes within the principles in a way that dictates tools, methods, and practices. They also acknowledge a few key players. They list sponsors, developers, and users. That incredibly shortlist does encompass everyone that they need to worry themselves about during development. The sponsors, or Product Sponsors, stand as the bridge between the company and the developers, while the users must always be on everyone's mind.

While this principle doesn't explain or elaborate on the agile processes discussed, it does go without saying that they're referencing the major advancements made by the people behind the Agile Alliance. They're looking at SCRUM and similar process tools and team management tools to reinforce the need for constant pacing and consistent communication between the three involved players. Although the users don't have someone speaking for them directly, both developers and the Product Sponsors must strive to give voice to the user creating a delicate check and balance.

This principle is another that sees overuse across many industries. Agile processes don't involve standing at every meeting. Just the same, telling a marketing team that they're going to SCRUM won't mean very much to them at all. The purpose of this principle is for software development, and that is where it should stay.

Chapter Six

Principles Which Define and Shape Project Management – Part 3

The final principles do take an authoritative stance, in that they either lend themselves towards a significant perception of software development or that they cite a specific set of behaviors. Although the previous principles are guiding, it seems that towards the tail end of the principles, there is less wiggle room or opportunity for widespread application.

Principle Nine

"Continuous attention to technical excellence and good design enhances agility."

This principle covers a particular note of common sense. If you focus on good design and technical excellence, then you'll be able to build up the level of agility. However, when you start breaking into what this principle actually stands for, you'll see once again that there is a much deeper root to making this statement.

First, this principle ties in the concept of continuous attention to the technical and design aspects of software development. The Agile Alliance aren't using this principle to say that they need to continuously focus on working quickly, or efficiently, or monitoring their progress. They are essentially saying that if they always move towards good design as well as worrying about the technical elements, they can pivot and respond to change more quickly.

Second, it calls attention to the flexibility of agile. This principle brings some clarity in using the word 'Agile' as a descriptor and brings to light that it is a spectrum. For example, you can use Agile tools or methods such as SCRUM and still have room to enhance agility.

Finally, this statement brings three things into focus and essentially rules that nothing else matters. Continuous attention, technical excellence, and good design are the three things that lead to enhanced agility. Without these things there, you will simply be using Agile tools, rather than the Agile principles.

That notion there that teams can use Agile tools without the Agile principles is something worth noting because it's sparked much debate. As mentioned at the beginning of this book, Agile is not LEAN or Six Sigma or any of the numerous project management philosophies or methodologies. Instead, Agile is a collection of principles and values, which should fuel the tools associated with the title. However, that often gets put the other way around.

The agile alliance used this principle to outline that the focus on excellence and design is the car while the tools used are the horse.

Principle Ten

> *"Simplicity – the art of maximizing the amount of work not done – is essential."*

Without a doubt, this is one principle, which can apply across many different industries, teams, and work methods. It's the age-old, *"Work smarter not harder,"* which fueled the industrial revolution, led to many assembly-line style factories, and even now is lending itself towards industrial automation. This principle is the one time that the Agile Alliance acknowledges similarities between manufacturing and development. The less you do, the better you can deliver in what you do.

Simplicity, however, does mean a few other things for software developers, including limiting chaos. During the software development process, it is nearly impossible to work on certain aspects together. You simply have to trust that the other people on your team are doing what they're supposed to and doing it well. When you simplify each process to its lowest factor, you can then ensure that everyone will be working towards a collective goal. These teams also work to minimize the work that is currently in progress. That is one element of SCRUM meetings in that the team works together on pieces of the project, and only moves on to the next piece when all the tasks for the first segment are complete. At first blush, this might seem to slow down the process substantially. However, you're giving each team member ownership of some vital but rather bite-sized chunk of the overall goal. When doing this, the team can accomplish what they're working on, then come together to help anyone who isn't ready to move forward.

Another factor of this principle that comes into play for software development teams is that the learning process of knowing what is or is not essential. When you're first learning how to perform a certain function within software development, it is incredibly easy to overcomplicate aspects of your work. However, you may recall from the manifesto that the Agile Alliance declared that they would learn by doing. The tenth principle gives the opportunity for growth and self-awareness. If you identify that you are overcomplicating any aspect of your work, you can turn to your teammates and ask, "Is this necessary?" or realize yourself that something is not. In many ways, this principle gives team members the opportunity to ask for help and to avoid wasting their time. Eventually, if everyone continued in the way they thought was best without this understanding of simplicity, the development process could come to a screeching halt when various aspects don't fit together. When working in a less than simple manner it's difficult for teams to stay on the same page, it's difficult for them to create a product that feels cohesive to the end-user, and for the team to understand what they're working towards.

Principle Eleven

"The best architectures, requirements, and designs emerge from self-organizing teams."

Was this a big slap in the face to the many micro-managers of the business world? Possibly and probably. Developers are often cut from a slightly different cloth than the people who rise to the top of corporate ladders. Although it's difficult to make these blanket statements without some backlash. However, when you look at the core functions, responsibilities, and work environment, it's easy to see that product management and software development jobs attract very different people.

For example, software developers often work under high-pressure, and that is something that they share with top-tier managers. However, software developers are often creators which lead projects and that results in high-job satisfaction despite the high-pressure environment. Whereas product managers often have to work with more human elements and soft skills to manage a team of staff who excel in a technical area where they have little or no experience. Product managers need to be able to lead and strategize for aspects, which are completely unknown to them. While software developers often become experts or have some degree of mastery with their everyday tools.

At some point, however, product managers need to step back and allow software development teams to do what they do best. This principle explains that no matter the framework, architecture, or structural organization method at play, the team itself needs to determine the method of organization that works best for them.

Principle Twelve

"At regular intervals, the team reflects on how to become more effective, then tunes and adjusts its behavior accordingly."

Did they save the best for last? This principle is one of the few that gives very tangible advice and does lend itself more as a tool. As one of the guiding principles, it is present in many Agile tools and methodologies, and it does, again and again, help teams manage themselves with high levels of efficiency.

What the principle doesn't explain is that during these meetings, the focus in on the project at hand, not just the dynamics of the team. As a self-organizing team, an agile group will take responsibility for organizing themselves and the imploding their processes. However, the product manager should be part of these meetings as well. Not only should the team focus on consistently improvising their effectiveness but that they should also look for small ways to "tune" their actions and interactions.

Given the scope of Agile projects, it's vital that the teams be able to meet and discuss improvements without disrupting the internal aspects of the team. For many, this principle is easy to understand and difficult to implement. Process improvement is a touchy subject as it often comes paired with criticism or insight, which can upset many within the group. You can change the circumstances and situation around the reflection, and you should. If you feel at any point that team reflective will have negative repercussion or backlash; then you need to evaluate your approach. This principle does not say to meet as a team and criticize. It says to adjust behaviors accordingly in order to become more effective. As always, the central theme comes back to value for all involved.

Should this principle apply to software development only? No. There is a lot of opportunities to implement this principle in different industries and teams. However, it does really come down to self-organizing teams. Imagine if your direct manager brought your department together and began assessing each person's performance. As a group, which had roles, assigned to each person, it's possible and likely that someone on that team feels their skills could serve different purposes more effectively. In these situations, a team reflection on behavior wouldn't be productive for efficacy or efficiency. This principle does really resound only to self-organizing teams, and Agile teams lead the way in that mindset. Few other self-organizing teams exist, and when you look at traditional project management philosophies such as Six Sigma, it's clear that project management is not often self-organizing.

These principles rule the foundation of Agile, and each gives something special towards their four values. The values can have specific ties to various principles, which is why the explanation of the principles came first. Although the Agile Manifesto follows the road map of introductory proclamations, values, concluding sentiment, and then principles for someone new to Agile to understand, it is easier to grasp the principles first. The Manifesto itself is a blanketed outlook on project management, but with a foundational knowledge of the principles, you can see the connection between the Agile Alliance's values, project management, and software development.

Chapter Seven

Agile Manifesto Values

The Agile Manifesto took hold and focus on only four primary values. In all of their daily duties, core job functions, and expectations to meet, they summed up the most critical aspects of software development in four short lines. Together the Agile Alliance cut through the most apparent elements, which are essential to the business people, involved such as Product Owners or product managers. However, they created a much clearer picture of what software development team needs to focus on to succeed. As part of their manifesto, they kept everything very short and left little room for manipulation or scrutiny. The lines, in fact, read so directly that they more or less tell everyone else what will and will not happen on a successful software development team.

It's, of course, worth mentioning that these all position the daily activities of a software development team by priority. As explained earlier, the closing statement of valuing items on the left more than the right gave explicit instruction as to what was a software developer's priority.

Looking at the very first stated value, the manifesto reads, "Individuals and interactions over processes and tools." That statement means that they value the items on the left, or individuals and interactions, more than they value tools and processes. Up until the mid-2000s when the Agile Alliance met, the business world had been engulfed in project management techniques. Although the Agile Alliance didn't know they were creating yet another project management philosophy, they did know that there had been enough LEAN and Six Sigma talk. Many of these men had led projects and worked as project managers. They knew that eliminating waste or focusing on perfection would only lead software teams into dismay. The focus needed to be on the people involved. Software development is a team effort. Without recognizing the many parts of the team, the software will not deliver on the quality or expectations of the managers involved. The mention of interactions here brings to light the need for quality communication as well. Yes, communication tools such as SCRUM have an integral part in Agile. However, if the dialogue isn't meaningful, if the information isn't correct, and if the interaction isn't positive, then it defeats the purpose of using the particular tool. Agile does not have any tools, which are cookie-cutter or continuously stamp out the same results. Even the communication tools employed in most Agile projects require careful handling and implementation.

The second value reads, "Working software over comprehensive documentation." After the Agile Manifesto was published and disturbed throughout many industry leaders, the management side of software development began to understand the arduous process of documenting software development. Changing needs, developments, and coding alterations can mean more time spent documenting the process than actual programming. In fact, it was one of the primary reasons for the onset and continuation of the application development crisis. Not only were companies calling for extensive documentation, which was impossible to produce and maintain, but this requirement led to inaccurate documentation. What's possibly more frustrating for software developers is that the importance of documentation was set out in NATO during the first software crisis. In the early days of software, development documentation was necessary to correct faulty reasoning, test the design, and to coordinate with other team members. By the time of the mid-2000s aspects of development such as debugging and working with a flexible design had been sorted out. Documentation in abundance was no longer necessary and in many companies documenting the process was a waste of time and other resources.

Now, Agile is not particularly anti-documentation. The essence of this value is that it is not more important to have documentation than it is to have working software. Product Owners and project managers are notorious for not being able to prioritize the importance of aspects of a project. When looking at this issue, the Agile Alliance broke down and asked the hard questions such as, "Is having the software working, or documentation of why the software doesn't work, more important?" They answered the question. Clearly, working software will always rank above documentation. Now there are still aspects of their projects that are present and mandatory. For example, a change log or backlog is useful in helping identify times or changes that cause software function to stop working. These logs now are much simpler than what documentation they used to be before Agile. Essentially a change log should reference the code or programming adjustment and have a date. If after that change the software stops working, then something went wrong.

Now, there is no strict guideline on what is or is not appropriate in Agile documentation. When working with your team, you should look at a few factors that come straight from the Agile principles.

Ask the team if the documentation is:

- Necessary
- Useful
- Beneficial for communication outside of the team
- Present value to the team and product owner

Documenting any unnecessary details will not only waste the time of the team member but also waste the time of any reading through the documentation. The team should also give consideration as to who is reading the documentation in the future tense. Are they writing documentation for other developers who may create updates, patches, or fix errors? Or, are they writing for the end-user and product owners? These are all aspects that make documentation more valuable, but again, in the end, documentation is never more valuable than functioning software.

The third value presents that customer collaboration is more critical than contract negotiation. This value is confusing because, through project management, you've learned that the customer could be any number of people. For user design professionals, the customer is always the end-user, and for coders, the customer may be the product department of their company. Envision it this way, when developing Adobe Acrobat, did the team focus more on, and collaborate with, their product management department or their intended users? When looking at the entire suite of tools in the Adobe Acrobat family, there were more than ten developers behind these tools. Because the purpose of Adobe development is to create software, it's likely that they used their product management department to collaborate with their intended end-user, a blend of the options mentioned above. This all starts at the very beginning with contract negotiation. Unlike other projects that involve project management, there is often very little input given throughout the development. Instead, the contract should clearly lay out the expectations of the end-product and the team's behavior along the way. That means that along with aspects such as deadlines and pay, are the more concept-based aspects of the project's goals.

Historically in project management, the focus was always put on the contract deal. How much would each person get out of the project and how much would they have to put in? These were the driving questions. Negotiations are often brutal, but thanks to the Agile Alliance enlisting this value, software development negotiations are no longer battles. They instead are collaborative efforts to identify what is necessary to complete the job in a way that makes the ideal result possible.

Instead of a few people getting together in the beginning and issuing a list of demands, this Agile value puts in a different script. The collaboration brings in the customer at the end of each 'sprint' and allows for changes. These sprints or segments are usually in the contract as milestone agreements. Then the customer can offer insight, inform the team of environmental changes, or the team can notify the customer of changes, which impacted their work. In the end, this approach to contract creation has resulted in higher-value products because the developers aren't working to meet one end. Instead, they are working to create something that fits the customer's needs, not just what the customer thought they needed.

The final value and perhaps the most present driving point within the Agile manifesto is, "Responding to change over following a plan." Project management systems and methods often leave little wiggle room for change. They instead take an approach that relies on drive, perseverance, and headstrong determination. Complete the job until it's done, is the mentality that rules over many Six Sigma, or LEAN teams. However, that's not the case for Agile. They used this value to make the development of a journey rather than a destination.

When you work in an industry that has significant advancements every few weeks, you have substantial room for external factors to uproot your entire project. Then when you look at the internal workings of the team and can see that each is personally learning quickly, there are many opportunities for internal factors to onset change. One day a developer could walk in and say, "Hey I just learned about this last night, and it's going to make the design more user-friendly, the system run more efficiently, and we just have to use it." What can the team say in response? The value of responding to change makes it easier for teams to say yes towards something that will result in a better product. From the example stated above, a team focused on hitting their deadline and sticking to the plan would quickly say "No." But not taking the initiative on this new knowledge may outdate their software before it even hits the market. Another team could be working and building something with that advanced knowledge and deliver their product, leaving the initial team sitting in the dust.

Does that mean that Agile teams rush in without a plan? No. They do plan, and they look forward towards reaching key milestones.

However, they take a much more sporting approach to their plan. A team may hit their respective field with the intention of scoring points in various ways. However, given the experience and abilities of the other team involved and weather conditions that plan could fall apart in seconds. Software developers are all too aware of this type of issue. So, Agile projects will often have plans A through D and know that all of those plans could not be put into use, and they may have to manufacture a plan E on the fly. Working this way, however, has turned out some outstanding work in recent year.

Agile teams often have a method for how to systematically change their plan. There are various methods, which befit different knowledge and experience levels for any project. These methods allow them to continue working, prioritize the changes, and implement their response to the change quickly. One of the key aspects of an Agile change response to avoid stopping any work wherever possible, and to begin working with the change in mind immediately.

When looking at these values as a whole, it's clear that there are many opportunities for Agile teams to succeed. After the initial publishing of the manifesto, there were many varied responses. From the software developers' side, there was positive and negative feedback. Many believed that failing to stick with an initial plan would result in never completing a project. While from the business perspective, it seemed that Agile teams would never be happy with their work or would be under too much stress from constant change. In many cases, the exact opposite has happened. Software developers are reporting higher than normal job satisfaction rates, and more than anything else is completing projects left and right. In fact, on the Forbes list of jobs with the highest satisfaction, software developers came in as the sixth most satisfying career. A good portion of that satisfaction may lie directly with the Agile Manifesto. Few other positions in any company have such well-thought-out or clearly explained values. These values help even the new people entering the world of software development understand that the customer and the software are always the most important thing in development. The other aspects of team dynamic, planning, and tools only play a part in making software, which is valuable to the customer. You can put any of these values into your work daily and see an impact on the type of work that you produce.

Chapter Eight

Various Agile Methods

Although the first mentions of Agile came about in 2001, there was much more talk about the many tools that would become part of the Agile framework. They are also often synonymous with lightweight or light software development tools. The Agile Manifesto was written by the thought-leaders that were behind many of these development tools, and the incorporation of them as Agile tools was not surprising.

When exploring the tools and methods that rule Agile, consider how they all come back around to the twelve principles. The principles, which govern Agile teams, should play a substantial role in any method used. Any method, which doesn't conform to all of the principles, is at that rate, not a true Agile methodology. It's a common issue that companies claim to use Agile principles but only actually use a few. In going through the principles, yourself it was probably rather easy to see that you cannot pick and choose which principles to use in your team. All agile methodologies should focus on customer satisfaction above anything else. Customer satisfaction should come from high-value software and well-mapped communication. Agile, however, does not refer directly to the completion of a product. In fact, Agile is much more about the journey of crafting a high-value product that functions outstandingly well. Two of the most commonly used

Agile methodologies are Scrum and Kanban, and each has earned its own segment. Here, however, you can read through the four most frequently used Agile methods outside of Scrum and Kanban. They are vital for any team's success, although every Agile team must carefully choose which methods are the best fit for them as part of their self-organization.

DSDM

It's the original Agile method, and it's still present among many teams today. DSDM is an abbreviation for Dynamic Systems Development Method. DSDM was first seen in motion way back in 1994, and that project was part of a Rapid Application Development strategy. Ideally, the DSDM would have given software development teams governance and discipline to work in a way that allowed them to focus on value instead of the many other aspects of daily work. People still choose to use DSDM because it allows them to clearly define their goals and act on real benefits for the business. Benefits for the business is one reason why Product Owners will urge their teams to use DSDM methods again and again.

DSDM does come with its own set of principles, and they all align clearly with the twelve principles of Agile.

The eight principles of DSDM include:

- Collaborate
- Deliver by the deadline
- Don't compromise quality
- Focus on business needs
- Build incrementally from foundations

- Develop iteratively

- Continuously communicate

- Control

As DSDM rose and the use of it spread outside of software development teams and into systems development as a whole the term changed. Now, DSDM does not specifically refer to the original Dynamic Systems Development Method, but instead will often have "Driving strategy, delivering more" attributed to the acronym. The "Driving strategy, delivering more," has become the mantra for DSDM as Agile teams have proven, this method allows them to work more collaboratively and flexibly than many other Agile methods.

People often choose the DSDM Agile approach because it deals with the entirety of the project rather than only the communication or only the planning. DSDM is also applauded for its scalability and working effectively with both large and small teams. Given the governance of rules, DSDM also provides a bit more structure than alternative Agile frameworks.

To use DSDM, you want to start by segmenting out the business requirements and making them user stories. Understanding how different aspects within the business will impact the customer or user can help guide decision making. DSDM projects will constantly refer back to the business requirements and user stories for decision-making purposes. When experiencing change, the question will often come back to, what is the business requirement. This method relies heavily on not working unnecessarily, and by reacting to change quickly with one consistent method of change response.

After establishing the business requirements, the team will work together to set their priorities. Usually, the priorities will apply to the business need and industry demands. For example, the preexisting demands of user security and regulations, which require certain levels of security, will take priority over design. Then, the team will come together to work on the project in chunks while interacting consistently with the Product Owner. They will deliver, test, and provide the software for acceptance within a relatively small span of time. After each acceptance or milestone, the team will collaborate with the end-users or customers to identify any necessary changes. The DSDM loops with transparent feedback and necessary adjustments until the project is complete, the user is satisfied, and the software is ready for launch. DSDM focuses exclusively on the project, rather than looking at the lifelong needs of the software.

Extreme Programming (XP)

Created by Agile Alliance member Kent Beck, Extreme Programming or XP is everything you would expect. It is a methodology that relies on simplicity, team communication, and feedback. That ultimate priority is customer satisfaction, and it takes precedence before anything else. The XP methods are what drove many of the Agile principles. In terms of how to treat the team members and how to bring in late-stage change. XP largely relies on teamwork and the entire team must work together to essentially pull the work together, much like pulling laces tight. Ideally, XP will deliver a simply written code, which works well and allows the developers to continue improvement. It also looks at the whole process and how each step lends itself to various goals. Finally, it's one of the more Agile approaches. While DSDM is the original Agile method, XP takes the approach of cultivating respect and responding to change with a positive affirmation that the change will produce a better user experience.

You may recognize the visual model of XP. The symbol looks like a globe with text running down the right, and the lines denoting the circular shape and appearance of latitudinal lines are all arrows. The arrows and text give a quick visual queue for communication. Extreme Programming has substantially more structure than DSDM in that there's a clear loop or series of loops for planning and feedback. The aiding goals are to provide iterative, small, releases of the software throughout the project. With that methodology in mind, the many team members, Product Owner, and customers can all communicate and deliver changes without disrupting the already completed work. XP is also where many of the less software-development-minded Agile methods come into action. For example, one step in XP is to have daily stand-up meetings and measure project velocity. These activities quickly became present in workplaces throughout the nation, whether they developed software or not.

The rules of XP are as follows and always happen in this order: planning, managing, designing, coding, and testing. Then it loops back again after obtaining feedback from the Product Owner. Each rule has mini-rules, which help the team know how, and when to respond to change. For example, during the planning phase, the team will work together to write user stories. They will also schedule small releases, divide the big plan into iterations, and to plan the duration of each iteration. Then during the designing phase, the focus on aspects such as simplicity and creating "spike solutions" in an effort to mitigate risk. The project will go through these many phases for the number of iterations on the project. Other aspects of the XP method include pair programming, which is still very present today. Essentially two people work together to create the production code for a particular sprint or task. However, these two people won't be partners the whole way through the project. Partners rotate, and it helps ensure more consistent coding use and promotes communication.

XP is a continuous process method in which the team handles the entire project on a large and small scale daily. They will act on issues immediately while together working towards the completion of high-quality software. Because of the scheduled small releases, XP is able to implement code refactoring. Code refactoring is basically editing for code. The team will go through and identify ways to simplify or improve the structure of existing code, without changing the functionality of the software. In other Agile methods, there are thought-leaders, which look down upon this step and see it as over-developing.

Lean Development

Many times, the line comes up, "that's Lean, not Agile" and in most cases it's true. However, the project management industry leader, LEAN, couldn't choose to pass up its chance to jump on the Agile bandwagon. Nope, in the early 2000s, Lean Development Methodology claimed to fit together the principles of LEAN and Agile. The result was not so much mixing of the two project management principles and more of an adaption of LEAN philosophy for software development. Lean Development does focus on eliminating unnecessary communication and obtaining information straight from the end-user or Product Owner. The decisions are all left to the team, and they can quickly make simple improvements because there are no bottlenecks in the decision making the process. Of course, there are some aspects of LEAN that couldn't be put aside for the sake of software development. As always LEAN focuses on fast delivery, and sometimes that goes against the core of Agile. However, there is also the availability with Lean Development for late decision making and team empowerment. Much like XP's code refactoring, Lean Development adapted the LEAN waste elimination philosophy for code. Here software coding needs to be cut down to its most simplistic and functional form. Eliminating unnecessary code or code which does not impact the function of the software can make for a more efficient or lightweight program.

The Lean Development methodology uses five steps to implement all Agile principles effectively. The first step is to analyze the value of the customers and identify what they need and want. Second, the team must work tougher to identify the value and the value stream. This step relies on the question, "Where can we focus our efforts to create a functioning and valuable software?" Then the team will structure a workflow that minimizes waste, which often means developers working separately or individually. Next step is to get customer feedback. The customer pulls if far different than other methods of receiving feedback on the product. Even within Agile, there is some grey area in how to obtain and process feedback from the Product Owner and customers involved. To create a more efficient method of processing feedback, the team focuses on improving aspects, which will deliver the most value. In that vein, they may only listen to the most serious or problematic complaints and shelving other issues. Finally, the entirety of the project is reliant on the continuation of these steps. The process of perfection-reaching is about much more than just delivering a product. Often Lean Development projects will hit an early release but require much more work after their release. That said, releasing the product isn't the goal of a Lean Development project.

Establishing a sustainable and structurally sound product is the goal and that many take many, many, rounds of revisiting and simplification.

Crystal

Crystal needs a bit of 'teasing out' as it is not one method, but a family of methodologies, which divide by the size of the group. Crystal Clear is a method for a smaller team of no more than eight people. Whereas Crystal yellow suits teams between ten and twenty people and Crystal Orange befits those with twenty to fifty people. While the method you choose largely depends on how many people are present, many overarching aspects occur in every Crystal project. Crystal focuses on the people involved and primarily look at people, the community, skills, communication methods, talents, and interactions. Alistair Cockburn was responsible for creating the original Crystal model years before the Agile Alliance meeting. Cockburn knew that each team size needed something different in terms of communication and making sure that each person was recognized and able to play a vital role. The overarching or overlapping aspects that are present in every level, however, include close communication, personal safety, focus, easy access to experts, technical environment, reflection for improvement, and frequent delivery. Much like Lean Development, many Crystal projects will see early release dates, but with constant improvement afterward.

Frequent delivery, perhaps the highest priority for Crystal developers requires that they release the iterations frequently and on a schedule. For each release, they must design the code and test it, with the goal of releasing each iteration weekly, or at most, quarterly. Realizing this method gives a time frame, but still allows the team to react to changes in the project. The Crystal method also works around a reflective workshop. The workshop is meant to help the team modify their actions rather than their behaviors, although behaviors are often brought up here as well. Ideally, these workshops will take place every few weeks. They should identify aspects of the team that aren't working and processing, which isn't working the way they should. This workshop sends us into the next major aspect of Crystal software development, osmotic communication. This style of communication requires that the entire team getting together and for the larger styles of Crystal methodology, they use Close Communication. The goal of both is to get accurate information to flow quickly throughout the group. During these meetings, they do rapid-fire questions and updates on every aspect of the project that's in progress at that point. Crystal can benefit many different teams, but ultimately, it's not a good fit for every project.

These more commonly used methodologies or tools within Agile all deserve much more attention. The brief overview here, however, should get you started with a basic understanding of each. It's important to note that nearly all of these predate the Agile Alliance's meeting, and members of the Agile Alliance founded all of them. If there is any more proof that the Agile Alliance was truly a meeting of thought leaders, it is that they created the major communication and organization methodologies in play at the time. They brought together project management methods, which worked, for software developers on teams of nearly any size. Still in use today, project management perspectives such as Crystal and Extreme Programming have fueled many successful software projects. Of course, you must carefully consider what aspect of the methodology speaks most to your team. Look at the personalities within your team as well as the goal of the project. Then you can decide which methodology within Agile to use as your communication and team's structural foundation.

Chapter Nine

SCRUM

Scrum is possibly the very first thing that people think about when someone mentions Agile. It's no coincident, and this is the most frequently used framework that teams use. It provides the highest possible value for products, allows developers to quickly and decisively adapt to changes, and keeps them productive. Mostly, it's a project management super tool, and that has led to many companies using some core Scrum tools outside of software development. Scrum is very different from the other Agile methodologies in that it has a very strict framework, with specific roles and explicit events. There are rules in place, and there are right and wrong ways of handling change events. Product Owners love Scrum because they know exactly what to expect from their software developer team even when they're entirely new to development. Working with developers, as a Product Owner, can be a struggle, to say the least. Imagine working with a team that must create a product that you could not possibly begin to put together. Scrum uses a combination of face-to-face conversation, documentation, and breaking the project into tiny parts. With this framework, there is no room for issues with communication, or for overlooking some aspect of the project. It is at its core the truest to all twelve principles of all the Agile methodologies.

Scrum does have its own set of values that coincide with the values of Agile. Scrum Values include courage, focus, commitment, respect, and openness. The Scrum values were put into effect with the goal that it was possible for any working professional to have proficiency in all of these aspects. The Product Owners and people behind the creation of the project will likely know that they want to use Scrum. That decision to use Scrum before there is technically a team in place allows them to seek out individuals that they know can deliver on the many values of Scrum and Agile. The most important value here, however, is openness. Everyone involved must agree to communicate openly, and that includes communicating mistakes. Ultimately, Scrum uses these values to deliver a lightweight and easy to understand framework. Like many other things, though, Scrum is easy to understand and hard to master. The method relies on the Product Owner, Scrum Master, and team members to all work cohesively at every step. Many people don't know how to work this way or come from backgrounds, which required silo-based work. Scrums longstanding success record is all the proof that anyone needs though to see that it works. It's a system that only works when everyone is on board. And when that happens, you have the closest thing you can get to a guarantee for success. Before really getting into how to use Scrum and what tools Scrum teams use, there are a few definitions to cover. Over the years Scrum has taken on its own terminology, and although you may have heard many of them before, it may not be in the correct context.

Scrum

Scrum is the whole of the methodology, although people often use the term to refer to meetings, the team, or even the software itself. Those are incorrect because Scrum is the whole thing. It's the values, the team, the work put in, and the communication necessary for the project.

Scrum Board

Visual aid for the entire Scrum Team that will help them see the whole scope of the project and the sprints individually. They make information visible and make it easy to answer questions such as where the team is in development.

Daily Scrum

The daily Scrum is a fifteen-minute meeting that happens daily and allows the team to focus their work and reflect.

Scrum Master

The Scrum Master guides the development team while bridging communication with the Product Owner. They are also responsible for teaching the team or coaching them to understand and use Scrum or Agile values and systems.

Scrum Team

The team of self-organized software developers, Product Owner, and the Scrum Master.

Sprint

A sprint is a short event meant to accomplish one small section of the bigger goal. Usually, sprints will be for one month or even less, depending on the sprint goal.

Sprint Backlog

This backlog belongs to the development team, and it shows the tasks necessary to reach the goal for that sprint.

Product Backlog and Backlog Refinement

The backlog is a list of the tasks or work necessary for completion. The Product Owner controls and maintains this log. As the team completes each sprint, the Product Owner will refine the backlog.

Increment

An increment is a working bit of software that will add-on to the other increments. Collectively all increments will result in the final product.

Burn Charts

There are two burn charts, including a Burn-Down and a Burn-Up. The Burn-Down chart shows the work that is remaining in the backlog and time is on the horizontal axis. The idea is that as time moves forward, the backlog should move closer towards completion. A Burn-Up chart takes the alternative approach and instead focuses on the work already done in relation to time. Both charts give the Product Owner, Scrum Master, and teammates a quick view of their trajectory.

Many of these terms are only in place because over the years; teams have put their own spin on different elements. Ultimately, the Scrum founders Ken Schwaber and Jeff Sutherland put together the official Scrum Guide. The Scrum Guide contained a glossary and began to create consistent terms that every Scrum Team uses now. The Scrum Master does require a bit more explanation as it serves different purposes to different people. For the Product Owner, the Scrum Master will ensure that the scope of the project and specific goals are clear. Then they will help the Product Owner find techniques for backlog writing and management. They will also communicate the need for openness from the Product Owner and put together meetings for them. For the development team, the Scrum Master is a coach and a guiding light. They do not lead the team, but they do lead the Daily Scrum and ensure that the team has all the resources they need. Finally, the Scrum Master has a duty to the business. That person will need to explain and obtain buy-in from stakeholders and administrative professionals who take part in the development process. They are responsible for advocating for Scrum and ensuring the team is effective.

Moving on from the terms in action, the framework itself is something else. Both founders argue consistently that Scrum is not a standalone methodology that independently it cannot work. Instead, they insist that they were using the method of empiricism. Empiricism is a philosophy of science, and with that notion, that means that Scrum worked itself out of the philosophy of Agile and into one from ancient Greece. Ultimately empiricism coincides the scientific theory and mostly relies on experience-based evidence. After the necessary foundation, however, that's about where the correlation ends. Without a doubt, the two founders did look to empiricism icons such as Aristotle, or John Locke. But to say that the entirety of Scrum is empiricism seems too broad of a statement for teams to also implement specific tools and values. It would also be arguable to say that if Scrum were entirely based on empiricism, then the person with the most experience should be Scrum Master. However, that is often not the case as the extent of experience in project management, and software development is usually not in balance.

There are specific times to use Scrum methodologies and when not to. Many people consider these project elements as a call for Scrum:

- Extensive research for markets, technology, and product abilities
- Developing software and software enhancements
- Releasing frequent enhancements or products, sometimes multiple releases within a day
- Development or maintenance of a cloud or similar operational environment
- Renewal or sustaining of products.

Clearly, all of these are present in nearly every software development project. These elements acting as the Scrum calling card are why Scrum sees such frequent use. The exception is when larger teams come into play. Scrum is meant for smaller groups that are handling very complex projects. The small teams on complex projects work because of the three pillars, which uphold the team and process.

The three pillars of Scrum are transparency, inspection, and adaptation. These are all present among the agile principles, and for many, it's critical to understand that this is where much of Agile originated. For Scrum, transparency means that they need to use a common language and understand the definition of done. That need for transparency led the founders of Scrum to create the glossary of terms and the Scrum guide. Inspection calls for the team members to look at their work and documentation frequently. That with skilled inspectors, they can quickly change issues as they arise, or even before there is necessarily a problem. Adaption refers to the ability to pivot quickly, and that is done through documentation, planning, and the daily Scrum, as well as the sprint review. Because there are so many ongoing elements of

Scrum, it's clear that even if it was not the founder's intention, they crafted a complete methodology. Then, when the Agile Alliance came into being, they let that methodology become an integral part of Agile. Among the elements of Scrum are the team members. While the definitions of Product Owner and Scrum Master already have explanations, the development team does not. It's difficult to pin down one definition for a self-organizing team. The best way to look at it is that no one tells them what to do. The Product Owner can say that they are happy or unhappy with increments, or aspects of the software. However, the Product Owner and Scrum Master cannot say that the team has to separate the project in a certain way. The development team will come together and decide how to divide increments and such to promote the functionality of the software. They will rely on each other for individual skills and operations aspects. There are no titles, no sub-teams, and no exclusive partnerships. It's likely that many people on the team will have unique talents or skills and will need to lend those to various team members at different points in time. Getting down to the Scrum itself, there are a series of events. The strict series of events is one of the reasons that many argue that Scrum is a methodology and not just empirical philosophy. The Scrum events include the sprint, the daily Scrum, sprint review, and sprint retrospective. Together they make up a scrum, although these events will often play through on repeat until the completion of the final product.

The Sprint

As mentioned earlier, the sprint is just one increment of the entire project. So, there will be many sprints over the course of a project, and the team must work together on each one. To accomplish that, they'll meticulously plan out a sprint. Planning a sprint brings the entire scrum team together. Sprint planning will usually happen over the course of an eight-hour meeting, although the goal is to spend less time planning. The planning event answers two primary questions. First, what is the purpose of this sprint? Second, how will the team complete the work? During planning the team will come together and look at the next step of their project. They'll evaluate the past performance within the team and choose which items on the backlog fall into this sprint. The upcoming sprint will have apparent goals, and each person will take on a series of tasks.

After the planning of the sprint, the team will still respond to change. As with any Agile methodology, Scrum sprints are subject to necessary change or change that will create a more valuable product. That there are times, which call for canceling a sprint. The Product Owner is able to cancel a sprint, and no one else has that authority. When it comes time to cancel a sprint, it is because a change occurred which made the sprint pointless. Although it's not common, these instances aren't rare. As part of the Agile motif, change happens, and it happens often. Occasionally that change will lead to aspects of the project, not giving any value. This part is where the backlog refinement comes into play, and the Product Owner must go through and decide which aspects of the backlog aren't relevant and edit or remove them.

The Daily Scrum

The daily Scrum happens for fifteen minutes and happens every day. This is the time when the team will collaborate, calibrate, and communicate. Usually, if a significant change impacts the project, it will come to light during the daily Scrum. The team will look at the backlog, look at what they did yesterday and what to denote as the tasks of the day. The few questions that come up time and time again focus around, "What tasks will help the development team meet their goal?" Then that question breaks into parts give the time, such as, "What was done yesterday to meet the goal?" and "What will the team do today?"

The Sprint Review

Before a sprint officially ends, there's the opportunity to review and inspect the work of that increment. The adaptive nature of an Agile requires that the team constantly look out for the value of the final product. That is the purpose of the sprint review. During the sprint review, the entire team and the involved stakeholders look through together to see what they accomplished. There is also the opportunity to identify aspects of the spring that need updating with particular attention to the documentation involved.

During the sprint review, the Scrum team goes through what on the backlog are complete, and what is subject to change. A team can mark something as done, knowing that necessary updates are on the horizon. During the sprint review, one of the aspects that comes up constantly is marketplace change. Questions such as "Has the product design accommodated these needs?" or "Is the marketplace changing in a way that changes this project?" the sprint review should last for one to four hours and is really just about communicating. They aren't problem-solving or working on the structure of the project.

The Sprint Retrospective

The final step of a sprint is the retrospective. That the Scrum team will go through the last sprint and then create a plan to make improvements. The goal is to cultivate even greater success during the next increment. The teal collectively will go through with the Scrum master to make sure that the entire meeting is productive. This meeting isn't a forum for arguing or trying to pull in elements of the project that some people want to manage. The sprint retrospective does open up a lot of opportunities for people to try to grab control. That is where the Scrum Master must ensure that the team stays self-organized and that skills are put to use where they benefit the team most. Although the Scrum Master participates and provides insight, there is still very little actual authority. The sprint retrospective focuses more on the tasks associated with the people, processes, and relationships. At the end of this meeting, the team should move on and tack the next sprint planning session.

Scrum methodology does have some implementation for documentation management, and it divides the work evenly. Ideally, the documentation won't overwhelm any single person on the team. The Product Owner controls the product backlog, the development team takes care of the sprint backlog, and the Scrum Master should act as an aid to both parties.

When looking at Scrum as a whole, it is a very reliable method for project management, particularly for software development. It takes a massive goal and breaks it down into achievable steps while also focusing on the people involved.

Chapter Ten

Kanban

Aside from Scrum, the most commonly used Agile methodology is Kanban. Now, Kanban is not exclusive to Agile. The use of Kanban opened up the window for Lean and Agile to merge together. Lean-Agile does not always use Kanban, and Agile does not always use Kanban, but Lean almost always implements Kanban meetings or methods. So, what is Kanban? Well, it's one of the few tools to come into the IT space after the Agile Alliance meeting. Kanban was first seen in IT and software development in early 2007.

Kanban is a management tool that fits into nearly any industry, specifically manufacturing and product design. That is where Kanban and Agile came together in that product design, and software development are very similar. The word Kanban comes from Japan and means sign or signboard. The process started with Lean in manufacturing long before Toyota was known as a vehicle manufacturer. It's a visualization and management method for workflow. For Agile teams, managing workflow can be the difference between completing a job on time and taking weeks to catch up on forgotten aspects of a job. Kanban is a very effective tool, but much like every other methodology of Agile, everyone must be on board. Kanban also ties in "just in time," which means that things are built as customers demand them. This mentality made it easy for Kanban to fit right in with Agile. Instead of trying to build the perfect system, the development team could focus on what the customer's a need now and then figure out what they need later at a later time. There is no goal of creating perfect software. There is no goal of delivering above and beyond the expectations of the company. Simply to meet the needs of the customer demand and then to move on with another project. While Kanban does deliver a very interesting take on Agile, it comes with its own setbacks. Many Agile purists believe that operating with the Kanban mentality doesn't look out for the customer, and it doesn't deliver the best experience for the end-user. However, others within the Agile community would argue against that logic, saying that working software is the most important aspect of an Agile project. The two sides could debate it for a long duration of time, but Kanban is still present within the Agile community. Not to mention that Product Owners and business people love Kanban because they're familiar with the system. With Kanban, everyone in the company will have a better sense of the status of the project. Many business people will implore their teams to use Kanban, but ultimately, it's up to the development team to choose their methodology and tools.

Kanban uses four primary principles, and they overlap significantly with Agile principles. The principles of Kanban include:

- Use what you know.

- Work in increments and pursue change.

- Respect the processes and roles.

- Encourage leadership on all tiers.

Sound familiar? It's no wonder that the Lean-Agile relationship began so early after the Agile Alliance meeting. After the manifesto came out, manufacturing and product development leaders noted the similarities, and since then the presence became ongoing. Today you'll find that most established teams use Kanban. They may not use all the roles, but they will often recreate each project with the same template. However, teams, which often change, or rotate personnel may not choose to adopt Kanban. Kanban works best for static development teams or companies that use the same teams repeatedly. Why? It is easier for developers to put more faith in each other when they have a track record. Kanban gives everyone a clear-cut view of the work, which needs doing, the work in progress, and what is done. So, over the course of one or two tasks, it is very easy for everyone else on the team to see who pulls their weight. This breeds the level of trust necessary for successful Agile teams. It also creates accountability in a way that Scrum does not. In Scrum it is very much, the team is responsible for the success, and the team is responsible for failures. Getting into how Kanban actually works, you'll see that Kanban has a lot more opportunity for personal success.

Kanban has six specific processes, which the team must go through together. The first process is visualization, and it's the classic Kanban board. Many teams are turning to software solutions such as Trello, or full Kanban software designs, which show a Kanban board. A traditional Kanban board only has three columns, which read out as: requested, in progress, and done. The tasks then move from one column to another on Kanban cards. Kanban cards each hold one task. The task must stand along but shouldn't contain any "and" statements. So no, "design and document" that would be two separate cards. When you begin working on a task, you move it from the requested column and into the in-progress column. It's easy to spot bottlenecks and slow-moving tasks with this method. The Product Owner could easy look at the board and ask why anyone task has been in the 'in progress' column for so long. Which takes us into the second step, limiting the work that is 'in progress.' Although a team may work on many things at once, there is a limit. Usually, with Kanban, the limit of 'in progress' items are six or seven. The idea here is that anything holding up processes needs immediate attention. Allowing a task to sit in the 'in progress' column is a waste of time, and it means that someone isn't putting in their effort.t

The third process is to manage the flow. That means ensuring that the things moving into completion first are of the highest priority to the customer. Kanban relies on a pull-system, so if the customer doesn't need it immediately, then it can wait. The idea is that the urgency of the customer's needs will speed up the process for creation, approval, and release. However, it can make managing the work difficult. At least one person on your team needs to have high-level prioritization skills. Someone needs to identify which tasks have the highest value and push those through to completion first.

Following the flow management, is making process policies obvious. Unlike many other forms of Agile, Kanban has a specific outline for the documentation goals. Ideally, anything in Kanban should have a quick and simple explanation. Terms that are less common, or anything which could be useful, need documenting. The process policies clarification step plays a role in the documentation. But it also plays a role in team functionality. Kanban has not always had a learning focus, but when it came into the Agile realm, this particular step stood out. The idea behind the fourth step in the Kanban process is that people won't work on something that they don't understand, or they shouldn't. So, everyone needs to understand the common goal and how the team will achieve it. There is a lot of room in Kanban to respond to change and continue moving in a positive direction, while still focusing on one common goal. Making the process policies and expectations as clear as possible sets the stage for a successful project. It helps cultivate transparent communication and keeps the development team on track.

After the team comes together on clear policies, they implement feedback loops. These feedback loops help the team synchronize, and they very closely resemble the Scrum cycle. Kanban loops come straight out of Lean philosophy but put a bit of a twist on the execution. For example, daily Kanban meetings are held standing up. Why? The Agile belief is that standing up gives these developers a bit of a break from sitting down at a desk for most of the day. It gets their blood flowing, helps them wake up, and stay alert. Then throughout the meeting, each person gives an update on what they're doing and what they accomplished the day prior. These meetings always take place in the morning and should last for less than twenty minutes. Then there are the service delivery reviews, or sometimes called the operations review. These meetings usually take about an hour and should happen at major milestones, or once a month. If you were to compare Scrum and Kanban, the operator's review would be the sprint review. The very final step is the continuous improvement step. Because Kanban uses a pull method, the team is in ongoing development. The definition of done almost doesn't exist here, because as long as there is demand from the customer for more, the team will continue working together. Through continuous improvement, the team works to collaborate with the company to identify or preempt customer needs. The goal is to never be behind in development. But that means as soon as there is a customer need, the team needs to know.

Straight out of the gate, Kanban delivers many benefits. It allows teams to prioritize things that are important to the customer. It also allows them to change with little distress to any other work accomplished. Kanban teams will often create functional software more quickly than teams using other methods, and the business people involved feel more "in the know." Kanban usually comes with very little resistance as well. The team's workflow is obvious to everyone, and bottlenecks quickly become obvious as well. What's more, is that teams can implement Kanban with very little effort. Essentially all you need is a board for your Kanban board. Then you will need to get everyone on the same page and make the goal of the project clear. However, if you're feeling technologically advanced and can invest in some software, there are many software solutions.

Do be careful when diving into Kanban software; however, as many of these tools actually defeat the purpose of Agile. Some would go so far as to say that these tools make Agile fake, dark, or ineffective. In fact, these types of software solution tools have led to what is known as the Agile-Industrial complex, among many other terms, which refer to the same problem. These tools often claim to fully integrate into your system, track your development team's work, and monitor their progress. However, that undermines the trust, which should fuel all Agile teams. It also puts more focus on software than people or interactions. Although many of these software solutions are very simple and don't take away from the human element of the team, caution is necessary. Always look at the big picture and avoid tools, which claim to automate the Agile process. Because there is no direct

"Agile process," there's no way that anyone could automate it. Then when you look at Kanban specifically its driven so ruthlessly on users moving the Kanban cards that the process isn't automate-ready either.

So, does Kanban come with any particular problems? There are a few knowledge gaps, but fortunately, Kanban's system is direct and simple. That makes it easy for anyone to learn and to use. It is subject to some overworking or facing a bit of software overkill. Moving past those issues, Kanban is a lot of opportunity with very little risk to you or your team. When choosing your methodology with your team, Kanban deserves a fair amount of consideration.

But Scrum and Kanban are so similar, how you could anyone possibly choose between them? There are a few key differences between Scrum and Kanban. Namely, there are no time limits in Kanban. Sprints in Scrum last at most for four weeks. However, everything in Kanban runs in real-time. There is no "milestone" due date, simply work on what is most important as hard as you can. Then there is the idea of optional assessments. Because Kanban teams will likely work together for longer, they can opt-out of assessment meetings. After months or years of working with the same group of people, the period assessments may be unnecessary. Finally, there is no set speed or due date. Kanban is ongoing, and it's great for software creators that are looking to make something that will last for years with constant updates. If anything, it does seem like software is heading in this direction. Even Microsoft is working away from their motif of creating a new operating system or new software suites every few years. Instead, they're chosen to work on their current software and update the versions. Eventually, they will release a new OS, but you shouldn't be looking forward to Microsoft Office Suite 2045. Working with a pull system, it's so much easier for everyone involved in development to get what they need and right away. Users have access to functioning software with their basic needs quickly, and an ongoing stream of improvements following. For many people, that's a preferred method of release. Kanban is one methodology, though and if your team can't agree, then you should listen and consider the many other methodologies within Agile as well. Remember that the people and the interactions are more important than the tools or processes.

Chapter Eleven

Benefits of Agile Methodology

Is it possible that there are clear-cut benefits from a philosophy without processes or tools? Although you could read through the manifesto in an almost Doctor Seuss like fashion, it's a very serious document. The Agile Alliance didn't craft the manifesto to put some ideas out into the world without knowing that a few results would happen nearly every time. The ideas, values, and principles, which make up Agile do set the stage for many great things. Of course, you'll want to ensure that you're using Agile properly. Don't try to implement Agile and expect all of these benefits if you're not working in software development. Compliance departments would not be happy if their team turned in a half-finished report, with working increments. In most departments, you need to deliver finalized versions of whatever you're working on, not just a functional version of the deliverable. There are times also when Agile isn't right for your approach because of limited access to customers or clients. If you're developing blind, then it's best to release your absolute best, rather than to release the functional version and then improving it.

The many benefits of Agile hit home for software developers, and they include:

- Predictable delivery of milestones
- Opportunity to implement change

- Focuses on customers or users

- Transparency

- Risk Reduction

Predictable Delivery of Milestones

About the only predictable aspect of Agile is the increments, or in Scrum the sprints. It's not difficult to keep track of various tasks and goals within the project either which is a little bonus of this benefit. The delivery of milestones in one to four week periods helps everyone, even those not involved in the development team, know that they're on track. It means that they can release or test the software well ahead of time. It also means that each smaller division of the software is known to work and work well before moving forward. There is no giant risk for companies to put in months of work to learn that something is causing the entire thing to fail repeatedly.

This benefit comes from face-to-face communication and the high-frequency of communication. It is possible to implement predictable milestones without Agile; however, you've probably seen first-hand the requests for extensions or blatantly missed deadlines. The reason why milestones work so well in Agile is because the methods involved break down the tasks and small goals for the team rather than for each person.

To see this in action, we'll present this example. In a Scrum meeting, the sprint goal could be something like, "map out user interactions for registration feature on paper, begin drafting design." Whereas in a normal project management meeting, that same goal might sound more like, "Jim, work on the user story and preferred interactions. Anette gets back to us with feedback from last week's milestone. Jody, test the user design when it's ready." See the disconnection here? When the managers in charge assign tasks to people rather than to the team, there's no guarantee that each person is using their skills correctly. From the above example, Jody, or Jim may have better connections to obtain feedback, but because the task was assigned to Anette, those resources will go unused.

Delivery of milestones largely rests on the structure of a self-organized team. The team identifies what work they're capable of delivering, and then figures out the best way to do that work. With all of this in mind, the milestones become much more predictable.

Opportunity to implement change

Change adaptation was the onset for the Agile Alliance formation and the drafting of the Agile Manifesto. The crisis, which plagued the software development community throughout the late 1990s, came from the inability to pivot and adapt to change in internal and external conditions. Agile allows that to happen, and this benefit is the leading reason for adopting Agile values. Through each iteration, it's possible for the entire team to recognize the need for change and alter their plan accordingly. It's also important to note there that documentation does play a key role in realizing many of the benefits of Agile methodologies. Where may teams only rely on a backlog, that one bit of documentation allows the entire team to reprioritize primary concerns when faced with change. It also allows them to implement changes to the backlog items that are set for the next sprint or iteration. That means that changes can happen in days or weeks rather than months.

Focuses on customers or users

The ability to focus on customer satisfaction is a huge payoff for many companies. When working with an Agile team, the focus on working software and improvement with every release or sprint. It can extend the product lifecycle by releasing the product earlier and keeping the product relevant for longer. It's also possible to keep customers more engaged throughout the process. The focus on customer or user satisfaction is something that stems from traditional product development expectations.

A side-effect of this benefit is that your clients have access to the functional parts of the software earlier. So, when the customer can use and begin developing training for the software earlier, it means that the release will come in tandem with comprehensive training materials or troubleshooting. Ultimately the product is of higher quality and improved usefulness for the end-users.

Transparency

Saying that transparency is a benefit is a bit of a risk because it only works as a benefit if the members of the team exercise it properly. Essentially, it only works if the team makes it work. However, if the team members are working with an understanding of the Agile principles, then it should go without saying. Transparency isn't just about communicating openly, though; it's about making sure that the goals are obvious and making it difficult to stray from those original goals. Working with transparency will also require different levels of communication. In one example successful transparency would include the communication between the Product Owner and the administrators in the company, while the Scrum Master must ensure that the Product

Owner knows the progress of the project and help the team stay on task with their goals. It's a very difficult aspect of project management to manage, but it has a huge payoff. With transparency, everyone has realistic expectations, everyone is on the same page, and when it's necessary, people can ask for help. Without a doubt, transparency is a huge issue in traditional software development methods. In the waterfall method, it was common for no one to know what was going on with the development unit the development team believed that they were ready for testing. Then that often led to many people involved feeling as if they were misled or that the team failed in one way or another. Agile transparency starts with contract negotiation, customer collaborating and bringing together the team. Ideally, the concepts of transparency would be on the mind of anyone assembling the development team. Then, the team would work with the contract negotiations in an open and honest manner. They would provide what information or insight they could and be forthcoming when it was unrealistic or when the team wasn't sure of the information. Agile isn't about following a plan; it's about communicating what the product and the customer's need. Transparency is a must if you want Agile to work, and the presence of transparency makes the entire project more satisfying for everyone involved. In fact, it's so important that transparency is the one area of Agile that has tools in every methodology.

In Scrum, the task-board is the presence of transparency in that anyone could walk up to the board and see the stories, work in progress, and finished task. A Kanban board shows the backlog tasks, their status, and what is in testing or finished. Scrum meetings and sprint retrospectives also boost transparency. These meetings and face-to-face communication are built-in aspects of Agile that people often overlook. There are many methodologies, but each of them centers upon making sure that each member of the team can access what they need and communicate where they're at with their work.

Risk Reduction

Risk reduction is a huge deal for businesses in any department. Agile confronts the issues of risk head one by insisting that teams act transparently. But other aspects of Agile methodologies help reduce risk as well. For example, working in sprints such as with Kanban or Scrum, the small batches make it easy to identify and mitigate risk in real-time. Rather than working on a giant chunk of the development to learn of a gap in security or progress. The small batches reduce the risk of outrageous costs, while the work in progress reduces the risk of wasted time. Transparency helps reduce the risk of low-quality, and the prioritization of the backlog reduced the risk of lost value for the company. The risk reduction for Agile methodology is outstanding, and it makes it imperative for software developers to understand how to implement Agile whenever possible. Using Agile can help you protect your relationship with your customers as well.

When deciding if Agile is right for you, make sure that you look at the big pictures. Are you using agile to accomplish one specific thing, or are you looking for a development method that looks out for your customers? The benefits of Agile are big-picture aspects because Agile operates on the big-picture level. It helps companies ensure that the final product is something that their customers want, and something that they need.

Chapter Twelve

Disadvantages of Agile Methodology

Having an Agile approach to software development is hardly any terrible thing. However, there are a few disadvantages to many of the Agile methodologies. They can impact developers, the business people involved, and even the customers at times. Ultimately it comes down to the management of the project and the team, and how you accept various trade-offs of using different methods. For example, using Kanban when there are few members of the team who understand Kanban will likely lead to a severe loss of time to adjust for the learning curve. The disadvantages of Agile are many, but nearly all of them are avoidable or preventable, and it depends solely on the team's approach and understanding.

Major drawbacks of Agile can include:

- Longer projects
- Many demands on clients and developers
- Lack of design effort
- Resource planning
- Done and finished are different things
- People get sidetracked
- Technical debt

Too Long Projects

The sprints are short, but the projects are long. That extent of commitment, the many face-to-face meetings, and close cooperation makes for long projects. While a sprint surely won't run longer than one month, a two-month project can quickly become a six-month project. However, it's not just meetings, which extend the projects out. Remember that these meetings are vital for the software to meet user needs. The issue is that the close cooperation and the agreeable nature towards change make it so that the developers will often add numerous features or aspects to the software. The goal here is to ensure that the user expectations are met and that the team creates the best software that they can. However, the time and energy involved aren't always necessary. Teams need to take a step back and identify if what they're doing is necessary. Refer back to principle seven, *"Working software is the primary measure of progress."* Many teams lose sight that there's a focus within Agile on the goal of working software. Adding in the unnecessary can make a better product, but it can also lead to a much longer project. Working in increments, which is standard for nearly all Agile methodologies including XP, Scrum, and even Lean, can make it easy for a project to feel short when in actuality it's gone long past its completion date.

To avoid doing projects unnecessarily long, ensure that everyone on the team avoids adding aspects to the project, which aren't necessary. It's entirely possible for the development team, which stays on for updates and new rollouts to bring in advanced features and ideas in the months following the initial release. Then it frees up the rest of the team to work on other projects.

Too Demanding

Is it possible for any development project to be too demanding? Yes and no. This problem is not limited to software development, and it is specifically a problem for any team responsible for creation. It's also a problem of perception. What is too demanding for one person is a normal amount of work volume for another. The underlying root of this issue comes from one or two-person Agile teams. If there is more work than people, then it's not fair on anyone and the purposes of Agile will extend the life of the project, put more strain on the developers, and more strain on the clients as they rush towards a release. Clients then must learn the software and determine if it's of a quality that they can support.

The best way to mitigate this issue is to focus on collaboration early into the project. Scrum is one of the top methodologies in Agile because of this issue. When working with Scrum, the team meets at the beginning of the project to design the scope of the project. Then the development team breaks that into sprints, and the full team meets at the end of every sprint. Even with very small teams, Scrum can help Product Owners and clients understand what they're getting and what their team is working with in terms of staff.

Lack of Design

This perceived problem does come with a set of disadvantages for the Product Owner and the clients. Although the foundation of Agile is trust, it is very difficult to execute. Asking your client's to trust a team they've never worked with before is hard for anyone. The Product Owner must also trust the team and for them working with the administrative side of the project can be difficult. Before Agile, with heavyweight software development, teams used the waterfall method. With that method, the administrative side was able to see the complete design before the work started. They knew exactly what they were getting, and they had an idea of what the final product would look like. However, when it comes down to Agile development that is not the case. The design is done per sprint, although the development team will often have a very rough sketch of the final product.

The solution to this issue is communication. When the administrative side of the Agile process worries, they should convey that to their development team. Make requests, ask questions, but mostly, ask if they're confident in their product. Trust is vital, but that doesn't mean that you can't communicate. As a client or Product Owner, Agile allows you to have a level of involvement. However, that doesn't mean that you can't communicate, and many Product Owners or clients involved in an Agile project don't understand that aspect. There is not a lack of design, but often a lack of communication about the design as it unfolds.

Resource Planning

Where other disadvantages are just veiled minor issues, resource planning is a major issue. Imagine if someone in the Marketing department approached their managers and said that they could develop a winning marketing strategy. But they had no idea what it would cost in terms of acquiring sales copy, ads costs, or the time to complete it. That is essentially Agile. While Agile's flexibility makes way for many opportunities, the primary issue that teams face is resources planning. Companies do not like operating this way, it makes executives uneasy, and essentially, only big businesses can get away with it. What is worse is that the bigger the project, the more unknown the needs for resources. There is very little to do to prevent or mitigate this problem other than to go with the flow. If you're working with an Agile team, you will need to trust that they are doing their best with the resources available. However, if you are part of the Agile team, you need to ensure that you're using the available resources wisely carefully. It's on every team member to not waste resources. If you're looking for ways to sharpen your resource handling skills, consider opting for a course or two in Lean processes. There are many overlaps between Lean and Agile, and learning both could be useful for everyone on your team.

Done and Finished are Different Things

The phrase *"Definition of Done"* or DoD gets thrown around a lot in Agile discussions because it presents a unique problem. There is no such thing as finished. Because these teams release software in increments, customers or end-users are likely using the product well before it's actually "done." Most users don't mind or care, or sometimes even notice because they have a working software, which just keeps improving. Often improving at a rapid rate, releases of patches, updates, and additional features make it so that these projects can last forever. The fragmented output approach makes it extremely difficult to know when to throw in the towel. Then you have the aspects of keeping the software up to date with other software and the hardware that users rely on daily. For example, the release of the Microsoft Office 2019 suite happened on April 9th with version number 1903. However, on May 14th, barely a month later, another rollout happened with version number 1904. The system was available, functioning, and users were happy. However, developers weren't done, so they kept working. Updates on 2019 continue, and with Microsoft track, record developers will likely continue refining the coding and tweaking small things until the next Microsoft Office suite release. Essentially, a Microsoft Suite will never be finished. It's largely on the development team and Product Owner to know when to decide that a project is done. This method of working is one of the things that comes up repeatedly as a disadvantage. If you're looking for a way around this, then consider using Kanban. With Kanban, you'll have a visual representation of the many moving parts of the project and the initial aspects as well as the added features, which came up at various moments during development.

People Get Sidetracked

This problem is present in nearly everyone's workday, but for software developers, getting sidetracked can cost the company a fortune. It can derail the team, the timeline, and on a small scale, it can derail the sprint. The problem comes from the combination of welcoming change, a core Agile outlook and having a minimalistic plan. Many blame the high-availability of getting sidetracked on a lack of processes. However, when you look at the many methodologies involved, Scrum offers a lot of structure for teams and does help them stay on track. It even gives some window of involvement for a horizontal check-and-balance with the Scrum Master and the Product Owner. If you're on a team that gets sidetracked easily, then resort back to the Agile principles and meet with everyone face-to-face. Focus in on the aspects that are sidetracking the team and identify why the team is getting off-track. Now, if you're the Product Owner or Scrum Master, then ensure that your team is working productively. Bring the focus back to the customer, not just what changing elements within the tech environment make it possible in term so features. Don't allow the surrounding environment to rule over the productivity of the team. Always come back to principle seven; the proof of progress is in working software. That is the goal, working software.

Technical Debt

Technical debt is a hot topic because although it is a disadvantage, it is not inherently a bad thing. There are times when technical debt is necessary to prove that the team should make a change or just to move the project forward. Technical debt is comparable to monetary debt and often cannot be repaid. Essentially, it's feeding into software entropy to accomplish a more urgent goal or solve a more urgent problem. There are two types of technical debt, and both are drawbacks, but at certain times, both are necessary parts of Agile software development. The two types include deliberate and inadvertent. Deliberate technical debt is almost always taken because of release date constraints or due dates. Often the tagline is, "We'll release now and deal with the consequences later." While inadvertent technical debt, is well, inadvertent. Often it goes unnoticed until someone on the team can identify the software entropy. Often if a team has to ask which team member is taking care of something, then they already have inadvertent technical debt. For example, if someone asks, "Who's layering?" then it's clear that something was missed or not planned for during the Sprint Planning. The best way to avoid inadvertent technical debt is to use Kanban or Scrum, although neither will guarantee that there is no opportunity for inadvertent technical debt.

Although Agile does have its drawbacks, they're not anything that is more or less noteworthy than the disadvantages of other project managing methods. As a philosophy, of course, there is a lot of room for error. It all depends on the application, and in true Agile form, it depends on the people involved. It's easy for anyone to step in and say that Agile leads to waste, or that Agile projects take too long. However, there are many Agile teams, which are waste-conscious and choose to work with the Lean-Agile methodology. There are also many teams who reach their definition of done on time, or even ahead of time. Whenever you're looking at disadvantages of Agile, it's vital that you look at the human elements of that team. Then you can decide for yourself if the team was responsible for the project failure of if the project failed because Agile doesn't have strict processes.

Chapter Thirteen

Addressing Agile Documentation Methods and Handling

One of the hottest debated topics among Agile professionals is documentation. How much is too much? How much is too little? How frequently should the team update the documentation, and whose job is it anyway? The issues around documentation do go beyond Agile. It was one of the driving factors that led the Agile Alliance to mention documentation in both their values and principles. Before Agile, there was simply too much of it, and a demand for even more. Companies wanted complete logs of everything done during the project and everything they would need to know to handle the software afterward. There is one definitive way of looking at whether the documentation is necessary or not. Ask yourself, "Does this document help someone remember something, or help the team communicate something?" If you answer yes to either portion, then you need that particular bit of documentation.

Let's tackle the first big issue when it comes to documentation, why is it so crucial to Agile developers if they don't 'do' documentation? See there's the problem that documentation is part of Agile because transparency and communication are at the core of Agile philosophy. However, people often see the value listed as "working software over comprehensive documentation," and see it as 'Agile doesn't have documentation.' Like many other issues in Agile, the problem comes from people taking a value or statement in as extreme a context as possible. It's true that Agile developers don't document their processes the same way as they did when they used the waterfall technique. Different philosophies and methods call for various actions and ways of doing things. It's a fundamental concept. But still, people complain whenever someone from an Agile team asks to see the documentation. Agile requires documentation of very particular aspects of their projects. First, they want the initial planning documented, intended sprints or stretches, and goals. Second, they want changes documented. Where did their plan change, where did their goals changes? These things are critical in helping the Product Owner understand what happened, as well as helping them realize why the direction or scope of the project took a turn. Finally, the documentation needs to serve the customer. Although many end-users won't ever look through version histories or change logs, they do serve a purpose for the customer. The company that purchases your software will likely need to create training material or courses for the software, how-to guides, and more. That means that Agile documentation aids the end-user because it helps develop well-structured or accurate training materials.

The brief mention of waterfall documentation does deserve a bit more explanation. After stepping back into time for a moment, you can realize what the Agile Alliance was working with and why the disdain for documentation was born. With the waterfall technique, developers had no reason to care for documentation at all. Instead of documenting along the way, the documentation was done during the testing phase. That created a ton of work. It seems to save work on the initial steps, but overall it makes it incredibly difficult, and it opened up quality issues as well.

For example, a team would develop software. Then it would go over to QA for testing and Quality Assurance review. Then as the QA representatives would identify tech errors, bugs, or issues, they would report it and continue with their documentation. When they were done, the project would go back to development for last-minute revisions and corrections. After fixing the bugs, the software would go back to QA who would then go through the documentation they had and correct anything to reflect the most recent version from the development team. This process would happen on a loop until there were no errors in either the documentation or the software. As you can imagine, projects could spend weeks or months, just going back and forth for bug fixes and documentation updates. For the developers of the time, that lag came down on them. It wasn't fair, and it wasn't reasonable, and that led many of the thought-leaders of the time to really hate the documentation process. They also hated that it was another department taking care of the documentation and that there was a time delay in correcting issues. Mainly, the waterfall method bred a lot of issues, which now, people don't see as problems because the problem is, for the most part, gone.

So, what are the methods and plans that work with documenting for Agile projects? Follow these guidelines to help document well, accurately, and within the Agile constraints:

- Document faster
- Document in Tandem with Development
- Discover Bugs, Report Them, Correct Them
- Everyone Documents
- One Person Should Manage Living Documents
- No One Works Alone

It's clear that some of these things are easier said than done, such as "document faster." However, when you put your mind to it, it's clear that it's part of the documentation solution. There are tools to help document more quickly as well. When using one of the set methodologies, you may be able to use a preexisting template rather than create your documents from scratch. You may also take notes while you're working to insert items onto the template or living documentation when you finish with that task. Which feeds into documenting in tandem or documenting as you work. Have you ever narrated what you're doing while you're working or doing a chore around the house? Have you ever watched a teacher in action? They explain what they are doing while they are also doing the task. It may slightly slow down the process; however, it can have a huge impact for capturing the event or task in its most accurate form. Many Agile developers have started using tools such as Dragon, or a screen and voice recorder. That way they can audibly voice their notes and later, transcribe those notes for formal documentation. Remember that the Agile Manifesto explicitly states that documentation is valuable, and it is critical that someone with technical prowess be responsible for creating that documentation. In that light, many Agile teams don't allow the documentation to go to an outside writer. Even a writer with technical experience may not understand the documentation needs or their private notes. Instead, everyone on the team is responsible for some extent of the documentation. Keeping the documentation work in-house also ensures that if a bug is found, as there is a bit of QA work going on here, then those bugs can receive attention straight away. Unlike the waterfall method, there is no delay in notification of bugs, and then a back and forth for corrections. The person documenting can begin to repair or correct the bug immediately and update the documentation to reflect that as well. Part of the reason that Agile team members can do this is because of the short projects. When working with such small chunks, no one on the team feels so overwhelmed that they cannot spend some time documenting. Documentation also helps the development team report the bugs to the Product Owner and explain changes during face-to-face conversations. It's one of those things that would come up during a Scrum Meeting. A brief mention of a found bug and the correction or change, which was made during this meeting, will suffice if everyone knows that the correction was documented correctly. That is where once again, trust comes into play. Team members must trust that each person is doing their fair share when it comes to documentation. However, documentation is the one time in Agile where one person may stand out for the duration of the project. Although the Product Owner will be responsible for their own documentation, the development team must find one person to control their living documents. For Agile teams that means checking on the accuracy, making sure they're updated regularly, and that they conform to the current changes experienced. Overall there's a lot to accomplish with documentation alone. To ensure that no one does become complacent and that all the work doesn't come back to the one person overseeing the living documentation, the team members will often work in pairs. The working in pairs holds each person accountable for their part of the documentation. But, working in pairs also allows people to rely on one another for ensuring their documentation is clear. It's easy enough to lean over to your partner and ask, "Does this make sense?" Or, ask them, "Is this necessary?" Documenting like this is standard practice across all Agile methodologies whether you're using Scrum, Lean, or XP.

However, there are a few deviations between each methodology that make documentation easier for the people involved. These tools have come to light over the years, there are some software solutions, but most focus on very easy to adopt best practices.

In Lean-Agile, there are few practices that immediately draw people into the practice. Practices such as avoid or eradicate duplicate documentation. It's far too easy to have multiple documents, especially when you have everyone working as a team, and everyone also documenting. The person handling the living documents should identify duplicate information and remove it or make it more concise. Another Lean method is to document late, that doesn't mean to deter documentation. It means to deter the official support documentation, in which you may take many of your existing documents. Then use those documents to create a rough outline or first draft of your support documents. Within Lean practices, many people enjoy looking at only executable information for documentation. For example, teams would only document information, which is detail specific to a single source of information such as requirements, design, or architecture. Rather than documenting generalized information.

Finally, perhaps the most important aspect of documentation is what Cockburn referred to as the team's "information radar." After learning a bit about Scrum and various other visual tools, it's easy to see that this is referring to that document. The information radar could include the backlog, but it will likely refer to the detailed documentation on a Scrum or Kanban board.

Agile has a lot of bad press when it comes to handling documentation. Although it's not as much documentation as the business people involved would like to see, it's enough. In fact, it is even better that there is less documentation because it makes the information easier to find and use. It's also more valuable information in that the developers themselves create it. Agile developers are by no means professional technical writers, but they understand what they are doing and their code better than anyone else. Documentation does play a major role in any Agile project. If you're not sure about your documentation skills, you might want to brush up with a technical writing course. Or explore some software solutions, which make it easier to record your thoughts. Then you can return to those thoughts later and clear up any confusing aspects or statements.

Chapter Fourteen

The Dynamics of an Agile Team

Is an Agile team, something that is actually attainable? Yes, of course, although with the slew of confusion around other parts of Agile it's no wonder that many people ask that question. The construct, purpose, and dynamics of Agile teams, however, is quite unique. Unlike other teams with hierarchical methods of communication and power, Agile fights against that tradition. There is little room for laziness, complacency, or even a lack of respect. In fact, unless you're using the Crystal family, which scales up for massive projects, there should only ever be three main roles. The three roles within an agile team include the development team as a whole, the Product Owner, and Scrum Master. Even when companies choose not to use the scrum methods, many will still adopt a scrum master. That Scrum Master stands as a bridge between the Product Owner and the development team. However, it's not fair to say that their role is any more or less important than the others present.

Starting with the scrum master, they often act as the project manager. They might or might not have direct experience working with the team. However, a Scrum Master should have some experience in development and management. They should feel confident in giving constructive feedback and overseeing the daily duties of each team member. They will monitor the scrum board help facilitate the care for any living documents, and more. The Scrum Master will not take part in the development itself. Instead, they will act more as a facilitator. They run the Scrum, Kanban, or other visualization board. They communicate with team members to break through bottlenecks and push tasks towards completion. The Scrum Master is a vital role, but it is hard on people. The taxing communication requirements of the job can wear people down. Then there is the aspect of translation. Similar to translating from one language to another, explaining what the software development team is doing to people who have no experience in development is mentally challenging. The Scrum Master will act as the guardian and champion of these processes.

Now hen iterating with the Product Owner they should take care to not step on any toes. While the Scrum Master will act as a project manager, the Product Owner is closer to the official title of the project manager. They need to communicate clear information in an effective way, while also not alarming the Product Owner. When the Scrum Master cannot control their communication, it can lead to a lot of distrust or concern for the final result. Which is the Product Owner's responsibility they are there to help the team course corrector to work in more efficient ways. For many teams, a fearful or suspicious Product Owner will spell doom for the entire project.

The Product Owner, occasionally an executive but more often a high-level manager has a key interest in this project. It's likely that they facilitated the deal for the sale of the software. Or, that they are overseeing the development of the entire product line. The point is that the Product Owner has a personal investment in this project. They will understand what the end result should look like and how it should perform. Additionally, they will align that product with the company's long terms goals. The Product Owner may want to be present at regular meetings. That sometimes includes Scrum or Kanban meetings. However, it's also reasonable to expect them only to show up when something goes wrong. The loose terms and boundaries for a Product Owner leave it very much up to that person's personality. For example, an experienced executive who's worked with software development teams before will likely not check-in frequently. However, a first-time Product Owner will likely want to be a part of the process. They may check in daily, or every few days for progress reports. If you're on the software developer side, or the Scrum Master side of this relationship, allow it to happen. Product Owners only develop faith in their teams through communication. The fact that a new Product Owner is showing devotion and interest in the team's developments is a good sign. However, there are occasionally issues with Product Owners who want to control the process. That is not the role of the Product Owner. If a Product Owner flexes their power to control every aspect of development, they will undermine the Agile philosophy.

Team members or the development team, make up the remainder of the Agile group. Together the development team may have front-end engineers, back-end engineers, videographers, designers, and even technical copywriters. These teams have a lot going on, but at every step, someone has some task to accomplish or role to play. That great variety in the team allows people to draw on various strengths when the need arises. It also allows people to work together towards building a better product. For example, many methodologies require that the engineers document their processes. That documentation isn't what will reach the customer or end-user. It will likely go through editors and copywriters first. When those copywriters come into play, it isn't just at the end. They will work with the engineers and designers throughout the process to document as they go. Everything with Agile is "as you go" and for the team, that means a lot of meshed work activities.

So, what about consultants? Well, honestly, consultants don't really have a place in Agile. Unlike Six Sigma or Lean, there is nothing to learn how to do with Agile. Yes, you may need to learn how to coordinate on a Scrum or Kanban board. But you cannot force someone to use values. If any consultants do come in, they must come in with the heart of a teacher. Anyone that comes in with the idea that they're going to change the people within the company doesn't understand Agile. If a consultant comes in with a slew of tools, software, and processes, then they likely don't understand Agile either. As mentioned previously, Agile has a lot of opportunities to go wrong, and consultants bring in that opportunity. Where many consultants initially go wrong is through assigning Agile homework. The Agile Manifesto echoes that the only way to grow in software development is through the act of developing software.

When you're getting people together, the first few things that you'll need to sort out are the overall goals, the needs of the customer, and the preferred methodology. The development team is in charge of clearly defining these factors. However, the Product Owner will be their primary resource for understanding their goals and customers.

Focusing on the customer is a team effort. Initially, the team will go through the outputs and find out how they can measure customer satisfaction. When working with your software development team, you'll want to look at the fulfillment of expectations. If there is a clear way to connect with your customers, then that's fantastic, and it's probably best done through the Product Owner. If there is no clear way to communicate with the customer, someone will need to dive into the research and learn as much about them as possible.

Then there is the concern of delivering value and continuous improvement. Continuous improvement is a major factor present in most Agile methodologies, although not all. The idea of working together as a team to focus on continuous improvement should be a positive event. When looking at Agile teams, there is not much room for criticism among the team members. The focus is always on the customer, so anything brought up in the continuous improvement aspect, should circle right back around to the software value.

With all these aspects, how does the team work together? The focus within Agile on people and interactions over tools or processes helps the team stay cohesive. It's no surprise that software developers report such high job satisfaction. As a team collectively, everyone is responsible for contributing to ongoing motivation and success. People often have room to "be themselves" rather than show up for work and type away for eight hours. Working together so closely allows many people within the team to grow personally and professionally.

If you're a Product Owner, or budding Scrum Master and want to put together a team, then you should consider a few aspects. First and foremost, look for high-level support. Your executive team and immediate manager should understand the personalities and abilities you need on your team. Additionally, you're going to have to do a lot of motivating in the beginning. When first putting an Agile team together, you're asking many strangers to simply, trust each other. You need to help each person prove to all the others that they are trustworthy. Unfortunately, the most difficult time for Agile teams is in the beginning weeks. When you're learning about what each person can do, and what they will or won't do, it's stressful for the whole team. Then you must plan for how you will handle mistakes. Mistakes happen, and if you have a plan for how to address your team, without losing respect or trust, you'll be in a much better position when that happens.

As you look at your Agile team, consider what is or is not working. Keep in mind that one of the fundamental principles of Agile philosophy is a willingness to adapt to change. You can take that mindset and put it to work among your team. Not necessarily changing your team's members, but helping them to adopt different mindsets, and approaches. You may need to also keep an eye out for those who don't respond well to the lack of structure. A self-organized team always has a risk of someone attempting to take control. Anyone looking to accomplish total power within an Agile team will leave everyone else struggling to use their voice. Always work with the Scrum Master, no matter your position, to ensure that everyone understands the purpose of a self-organizing team. There are no titles, and there are no 'team leaders' or 'assistant Scrum Masters.' The entire system works because everyone is equal, and everyone contributes.

No matter your position, your first Agile team will come with many hard lessons learned. You'll have to experience what it is like to work in a self-organizing team. You'll also need to experience the impact of communicating face-to-face daily and having high levels of trust between team members. Is it idealistic? Yes, but that is the point. Agile teams set the bar very high in terms of interactions and relationships. That high goal should motivate every team member to treat their teammates with respect and trust. It should help the teamwork with the Product Owner and Scrum Master in a respectful and trusting manner as well.

Chapter Fifteen

Implementing Agile Methodology

How can you start implementing agile methodologies? It depends on where you are in your work. As well as the condition of your environment and the construct of your team. For example, if you're working indirectly to your software development team, then you may adopt some of the Agile principles but not necessarily the Agile methodologies. If your team is built up of people with clear communication problems, who cannot respect the Agile principles, then it may not be the right time to implement Agile. You need to put a careful focus on how you will go about implementing agile methodologies and how you can best approach the topic with your team. Keep in mind that Agile teams utilize self-organization, and there must be no strict titles among the team outside of Scrum Master and Product Owner.

Additionally, each person within the team must understand the values and principles of Agile. They should also be able to showcase these principles in action. These concerns don't mean that you can't or shouldn't begin to bring in Agile methodology.

To start bringing Agile into your workplace, give a brief survey. Look around and see how clear the communication is between the administrative and development teams. Also, take a close look at how the members of the development team interact with each other. See how they approach each project. Many of the development team may be already familiar with Agile principles and terms. However, keep in mind how often people claim that practices or methods are Agile when they are not.

If you've decided that Agile is right for your team, then you should bring together a meeting or training so that you can get everyone on the same page. Use this meeting to lay out a foundation for your team. During this meeting or brief training, you will want to address many of the Agile misconceptions so that people don't come into the next project with any unclear aspects of their role. Explain how and why self-organizing teams work so well in software development. Also, look at how the team should operate within a time frame. Do you have a team of people who often meet deadlines, or does your software development team request extensions again and again? Then evaluate the core of the extension requests. Does the team need extensions to complete their work? Or is it to adapt to changes that were made late in the process? So many aspects go into compiling an Agile development team. Many managers or Product Owners will often use the transition to Agile methodologies to put together a new team. Ultimately as you transition, you will need to work with your team to set new standards and expectations. The Agile process, principles, and values are so people-driven that one toxic or rebellious person on the team could derail the entire process. Work with your higher-ups to address personnel issues or concerns that you have before you begin your first Agile project.

There are a few things that you can do to put together an Agile team that's primed for success. While there isn't a specific formula that leads to success, there are many prevailing aspects of a team, which leads naturally to success. Creating an Agile team is not an easy process, so strap in and get ready. Before you start bringing together your team, you'll need to lay out a few key aspects for personnel selection and strategies to set attainable expectations or standards. Work with the Product Owner, or if you are the Product Owner, identify the person most likely to take the mantle of Scrum Master. Together you will need to flesh out what aspects will be most important to upholding the Agile principles and value. Most leaders end up with three pieces of documentation, a checklist of virtues and values, a very detailed job description, and a team agreement.

The checklist of virtue and values should outline the standard values from the Agile Manifesto, your company values, and the virtues from the Agile principles. Some values and virtues that you might consider adding to your checklist include:

- Patience

- Adaptability

- Willingness to self-reflect on failures

- Willingness to receive criticism and feedback

- Positive mindset regarding change

- Positive mindset regarding simplifying processes wherever possible

- Communicates with priority on respect

You can craft this checklist in a few different ways. Some employers look toward the team members to fill in answers to questions that allude to these virtues. For example, instead of deciding for yourself if someone communicates with respect, you can ask a potential team member, "Is it more important to be right, or to be kind?" This can give you insight into how they would prioritize their own communication methods.

Moving past the checklist, you'll want to focus on the job description. Revisiting the job description for a software developer can be an arduous task. It requires going to HR and dealing with many people along the way. However, when you have the opportunity to include things such as, "communicate changes to the technology environment immediately," or "deliver sprint goals on deadline consistently," then you have more room to govern your team. From a Product Owner or Scrum Master standpoint, it is very difficult. Many people don't trust others on their team to do their job, and much of Agile relies on that very basic level of trust. However, that distrust does come from a place of experience. How often have managers heard excuses? How often have you personally heard someone say, "That's not my job," or more directly, "That's not in my job description." The power of including very specific language in a job description, specifically for self-organizing teams isn't about control. Governance isn't about telling people what to do; it's about laying down clear expectations. With the job description, you are telling team members that if they take the position, they must meet these expectations. Self-organizing teams often have these expectations and can still function to the best of their ability.

Team agreements are another thing to consider drafting. However, you and the Product Owner or Scrum Master may want to evaluate if it's necessary. A team agreement, from the view of many people, doesn't fit into the Agile motif of having less documentation. However, many project managers believe that if there is any question about the personalities on the team that a team agreement is necessary. Team agreements are social contracts, which help teams, perform at higher levels because it sets the tone for the project. Team agreements usually are the first thing that the team will work on together, which gives the Product Owner and Scrum Master a chance to see how the team can collaborate.

How can you get your team together to write a team agreement? After you go through everyone and have your team come together, schedule a meeting. Then divide the meeting into five segments. These segments will be to decide the tone, create a memory that the team will share, look for themes and connections, set priorities, and summarize the events of the meeting. Some of these will overlap with other steps of the project planning and dividing everything into sprints if you're using the Scrum method. However, this meeting and this agreement focus more on the elements of the personalities and communication abilities within the team. Allow the team to come together but ask that they set a time limit for each segment so that the meeting remains productive and short. Again, many people argue that there is no need for a team agreement because the Agile Manifesto should stand as a team agreement for anyone working on an Agile project.

Ultimately, the biggest obstacle that you'll need to overcome when implementing Agile in your company or department is trust. If you are the manager or supervisor, then you need to trust your staff to perform in ways they haven't performed previously. You'll also need to trust the others in your company on the administrative level as well. Your self-organized team that should operate on unbelievable levels and with high reports of job satisfaction relies on your trust. Give them that trust.

When you go through and have your team together with any documentation in place, then you can go to your next step. Consider working with your team to create a succinct list of the tools you will use. And decide which methodology within the Agile family is right for the project and get ready to release your team. The executives at hand may feel comfortable throwing around Agile terms but may not necessarily know what they mean or how to use them properly. Let these go and revert back to the principles of communicating respectfully and focusing on delivering working software. While it is vital that everyone on the team knows what is going on and how to use Agile appropriately, it is not your job to teach the entire company about becoming Agile.

Starting your first Agile project can be nerve-wracking for everyone in the company. It can cause a lot of unease, and the only advice that can be given to help in this is to over-communicate. Invite the Product Owner or concerned executives to watch a Kanban or Scrum meeting. Fill them in on how quickly your team responded to a team, or how the Scrum Master worked to bridge communication with the Product Owner to take a new step. Showing Agile in motion is the only way to help those who don't understand the process ease up and begin to trust the development team the way that you do.

Chapter Sixteen

Is Agile Still Present?

Agile was the hot topic after the Agile Alliance first published the Agile Manifesto. It rivaled thought processes in project management such as Six Sigma, and LEAN. Agile appeared in Dilbert comics, was present in discussions on sitcoms and today there is no shortage of Agile jokes. Most jokes and references revolve around the nature of hard work, long hours, or lack of documentation and tools. While all are true, some can be a bit self-defeating. With memes that read, "What day is it? Never mind, hand me a Five Hour Energy drink," it can make teams a little wary about adopting Agile. But is that even a concern anymore? Is Agile something you have to learn and implement and teach?

You do, and you should. Throughout the last ten years or so, it seems like the talk about Agile has died down a bit aside from the pop-culture references. Why? Because the tech industry has it's thought leaders. The thought leaders that wrote the Agile Manifesto are still actively working. Unlike other project management philosophies, there is no end-game or certified training program for Agile. Many people, specifically within the software development community, relate Agile to more of a culture than a project management system. With that mindset, it would be easy to see Agile drop out as younger developers come in with different ideas and goals. However, that isn't the case.

Many younger developers have learned Agile as their only way for developing so that Agile is not a choice or decision, but it's simply the only way that they know how to work with each other. This one meeting of minds changed the entire environment for technology developers. So, is it still present?

The biggest thing that calls into question if Agile is still present or not is the Agile Industrial complex. Like anything else created by great minds, Agile was subject to manipulation and inaccurate use. When the Agile boom happened, many software development companies jumped to fulfill the need for frameworks, tools, and process solutions. Anyone familiar with the concept of Agile, however, could quickly identify that this goes against the idea of Agile. The concept of having an approach without strict frameworks, tools, or processes allowed software developers the freedom to work in any way necessary. It gave them the flexibility to focus on results rather than following the next step in a process. The many methodologies, which Agile gave birth to all, fit the structure, and all have escape routes to accommodate change on any scale. The idea is that the focus was always on the team rather than the process. That no tool should ever be more important than how people work together. But, with tools, the software solution frameworks, and programs that teach the "Agile Process," this notion quickly took flight. Many companies, executives are especially guilty of this, would rather pay for a software solution and claim that their teams use Agile methods than put effort into learning about Agile. It's a struggle for so many companies, and it has a name. The Agile Alliance has noted this as "faux agile, "dark agile," but, more commonly, "the Agile Industrial Complex." The Agile Industrial complex became the term that described the state of Agile when people began offering Agile education or consulting. The issue here is that it deviates from the fundamental principles, but it does also deliver on a need. Executives and the other administrators who participate in the software development process do need tools to help them understand and monitor the Agile process. The Agile Alliance perhaps had one gap in their values or principles. And it was in that they didn't outline the usefulness of various tools for those people outside of the development team. However, the very first value, the "Individuals and interactions over processes and tools;" shows that they don't reject processes and tools. So, what does that mean for the companies that create tools and processes for Agile teams? Is it helpful or hurtful? Is it leading to the death of Agile, or the cultivation of it?

Although many argue, including Ron Jefferies of the Agile Alliance, that there is such a thing as "Manifesto Agile" when referring to tools. Such as using flexible tools to stand in as digital Kanban or Scrum boards. So, while there is some divide on whether there are tools, which can befit the Agile values, principles, and ideals, it's more likely that these tools distort that idea. Or, that the businesspeople involved in their use distort them to undermine the actual values of the Manifesto. The presence of these tools, and processes, and the distortion of the Manifesto have led many people to call the Agile movement dead. However, in reading through this book, you've probably come across a variety of familiar terms, project management tools, processes, or even just ideas. Agile has ingrained itself in software development, and the concepts that live within Agile were taking hold before the Agile Alliance came together. Without a doubt, the seventeen who laid out the Agile Manifesto had been hard at work for years trying to cultivate a sense of developer-focused software creation projects. These ideas will continue to exist long after the seventeen retire because of the massive change and availability they brought to software. If not for the

Agile Manifesto, and those thought leaders coming together we would likely still be working with the traditional waterfall methods of development and be years behind as we were in the 1990s with the software crises. Agile now does mean something different than it did in 2001. However, that change hasn't just come from the advancement or development of software and Agile, focused tools. Changes to Agile have also come from the many advancements in methods, planning strategies, and understanding of what the Agile values mean to different people. Regarding Agile as a philosophy, each company has its extent of implementing the ideals of Agile. Whereas if Agile were closer to project management processes such as Lean or Six Sigma, there would be fewer issues with Dark Agile or Faux Agile.

The core of Agile, however, seems to be very much intact. When you look at whether software developers are using the Agile Manifesto to guide them towards more user-focused or customer-focused software solutions, it's still in effect. Little has happened to sway Agile developers from working adaptively and collaboratively. That focuses on the customer involved. Yes, they buzzwords may have come and gone. The exercises may have been overdone in various other industries, but at its most useful state, Agile is still alive and well. Companies must question, however, if with the degree of notoriety that Agile has gained if it's worth it attempting to implement Agile and the Agile methods into their software development team. Honestly, the answer will vary by company, although most companies which work with software development should implement the Agile principles at least. Even if the company doesn't end up working with XP, Scrum, or Kanban, the principles in themselves can change the final impact of the work. That's not to say that companies should put in a half-hearted attempt either. Half-hearted Agile, often called Flaccid Agile, is in many events worse than Dark Agile or Faux Agile. Rather than using effective tools and slapping the Agile name on it, these teams are loosely following the principles and values. The result of Flaccid Agile isn't effective. Not simply because the team didn't commit to developing in an Agile methodology such as Scrum. When teams cannot commit to the principles of Agile, they are turning away from the customer. So, in a sense, every development team should operate with at least the principles in mind. Even when teams don't directly adhere to the values, which create a developer-focused team and environment, focusing on the customer is vital in any product development scenario.

How does this all fit into the developers that are learning and growing today? They are learning with much more complexity in their development teams and products. Unlike 2001, the software isn't often to serve a sole purpose but to serve many and connect seamlessly together with many other software solutions to create a cohesive environment of all-star software. There is also a higher level of business complexity. Companies don't look for developers that they know from job markets; they are willing to bring someone in and cultivate an internal expert. That means that these businesses are looking for a high return on their investment, and it leads many budding software developers to work unreasonable hours and under extreme pressure. Those conditions, however, do lend themselves to support these budding developers when they tell their managers that developers need self-organizing teams. Or, when a change happens to come forward and give a realistic manner of implementing the change and a realistic time-frame for delivery.

Agile is not dead, far from it. The principles and values have become so ingrained in the software developer culture that it would be difficult to eradicate them now. However, that doesn't mean that there aren't generally poor employees, unhealthy managers, or new tools available. If you're worried about falling prey to Dark Agile, or Faux Agile, or even Flaccid Agile, then put your focus on staying true to first the principles and then the values. It won't do any good to become so much of an Agile purist that you miss out on high-quality tools that simply weren't available in 2001.

Additionally, Agile purists may make it difficult for the team to work together. With Agile, especially in its more modern state, it's always most important to focus on the people involved. Look at the people you're working with, and what they can do to help deliver a better product to the customer. Those are the things that matter in carrying on Agile. Agile will no doubt continue to develop as the landscape of technology and technology development changes at lightning speed. Agile is the pathway to success for any development team because of the understanding that change is imminent, and the customer needs are the most important. Without a doubt, Agile will continue to play a major role in software development teams and projects. You should expect the values and principles of Agile to become standard across the industry.

Conclusion

Now that you know the very foundation and the modern news on Agile, you can move forward with expanding your knowledge through application. Work with your team and cultivate an interest in Agile tools or methods. Simply starting with a SCRUM or Kanban approach, you can openly engage your team in Agile practices. However, you do need to go beyond the practices. With the recent recognition of the Agile-Industrial complex, dark Agile, and dark Scrum, it's more important than ever to work with the principles of Agile in mind. The Agile Alliance came together to layout timeless values and principles to guide all software developers.

Don't break away from the traditional Agile principles or force them to work in industries, which wouldn't be compatible with any particular principle. Keep in mind that Agile methods and tools were created or best fit for software development. Although Agile is largely a project management philosophy, it is only directly applicable to software development.

The one thing to take away from this book, if nothing else, is the value system. As a budding software developer, you will no doubt come across many projects, which call these values into question. When working with the four values of Agile as your focal point, you can work towards consistently providing high-value software for customers.

References

https://en.wikipedia.org/wiki/Project_management

https://www.agilealliance.org/agile101/

https://www.liquidplanner.com/blog/6-essential-skills-for-project-managers/

https://www.strategyex.co.uk/blog/pmoperspectives/15-skills-project-managers-will-need-2015/

https://en.wikipedia.org/wiki/History_of_software

https://www.capterra.com/history-of-software

https://techbeacon.com/app-dev-testing/agility-beyond-history-legacy-agile-development

http://agilemanifesto.org/

https://www.forbes.com/sites/quora/2015/12/11/how-we-lost-the-ability-to-travel-to-the-moon/#1e1bfae51f48

https://agilemanifesto.org/history.html

https://www.smartsheet.com/comprehensive-guide-values-principles-agile-manifesto

https://www.agilealliance.org/agile101/the-agile-manifesto/

https://www.agilealliance.org/agile101/the-agile-manifesto/

https://www.agilealliance.org/agile101/12-principles-behind-the-agile-manifesto/

https://www.agilealliance.org/agile101/12-principles-behind-the-agile-manifesto/

https://www.agilealliance.org/agile101/12-principles-behind-the-agile-manifesto/

https://agileknowhow.com/2019/02/19/thats-not-agile-thats-lean/

https://www.yodiz.com/blog/agile-manifesto-12-principles-explained-for-sw-development-parti/

https://www.agilealliance.org/agile101/12-principles-behind-the-agile-manifesto/

https://medium.com/@agile42/introduction-to-agile-part-2-what-is-agile-f56103b9ad71

https://www.agilealliance.org/agile101/12-principles-behind-the-agile-manifesto/

https://www.agilealliance.org/agile101/12-principles-behind-the-agile-manifesto/

https://www.scrum.org/resources/what-is-scrum

https://www.youtube.com/watch?v=TRcReyRYIMg&vl=en

https://www.agilealliance.org/agile101/12-principles-behind-the-agile-manifesto/

https://www.agilealliance.org/agile101/12-principles-behind-the-agile-manifesto/

https://www.agilealliance.org/agile101/12-principles-behind-the-agile-manifesto/

https://www.agilealliance.org/agile101/12-principles-behind-the-agile-manifesto/

https://www.agilealliance.org/agile101/12-principles-behind-the-agile-manifesto/

https://www.princetonreview.com/careers/145/software-developer

https://medium.com/swlh/a-day-in-the-life-of-a-product-manager-4a11d106ffa5

https://www.agilealliance.org/agile101/12-principles-behind-the-agile-manifesto/

https://techbeacon.com/app-dev-testing/agility-beyond-history-legacy-agile-development

http://www.informit.com/articles/article.aspx?p=2246403

https://www.infoq.com/articles/roadmap-agile-documentation/

https://en.wikipedia.org/wiki/Adobe_Acrobat

https://www.dummies.com/careers/project-management/applying-agile-management-value-3-customer-collaboration-over-contract-negotiation/

https://www.dummies.com/careers/project-management/applying-agile-management-value-4-responding-to-change-over-following-a-plan/

https://www.forbes.com/pictures/mkl45eeilm/no-6-happiest-job-software-developer/#1d9ebf8b6186

https://www.agilebusiness.org/page/whatisdsdm

https://agilekrc.com/resource/168/what-dsdm-and-8-principles

https://www.testingexcellence.com/common-agile-development-methodologies/

https://www.agilebusiness.org/page/ProjectFramework_02_Choosing DSDM

https://www.xpand-it.com/2018/10/11/top-5-agile-methodologies/

https://airbrake.io/blog/sdlc/extreme-programming

https://www.castsoftware.com/glossary/lean-development

https://www.dozuki.com/blog/2016/08/30/a-quick-5-step-guide-to-lean-product-development

https://www.scrum.org/resources/scrum-glossary

https://www.scrum.org/resources/what-is-scrum

https://en.wikipedia.org/wiki/Empiricism

https://www.scrumguides.org/scrum-guide.html

https://www.scrumguides.org/scrum-guide.html

https://kanbanize.com/kanban-resources/getting-started/what-is-kanban/

https://en.wikipedia.org/wiki/Kanban

https://kanbanize.com/kanban-resources/getting-started/what-is-kanban/

https://codingsans.com/blog/kanban-in-software-development

https://www.digite.com/kanban/what-is-kanban/

https://www.sitepoint.com/how-why-to-use-the-kanban-methodology-for-software-development/

https://www.theverge.com/2015/5/7/8568473/windows-10-last-version-of-windows

https://www.romanpichler.com/blog/effective-sprint-goals/

https://www.seguetech.com/8-benefits-of-agile-software-development/

https://apiumhub.com/tech-blog-barcelona/benefits-of-agile-project-management/

https://www.boost.co.nz/blog/2018/11/agile-transparency-reduces-project-risk

https://www.inc.com/adam-fridman/the-massive-downside-of-agile-software-development.html

http://tryqa.com/what-is-agile-model-advantages-disadvantages-and-when-to-use-it/

https://docs.microsoft.com/en-us/officeupdates/update-history-office-2019

https://www.lucidchart.com/blog/3-disadvantages-of-agile-methodology

https://en.wikipedia.org/wiki/Technical_debt

https://techbeacon.com/app-dev-testing/why-agile-teams-should-care-about-documentation

https://www.sciencedirect.com/topics/computer-science/agile-manifesto

https://reqtest.com/agile-blog/agile-documentation/

http://www.agilemodeling.com/essays/agileDocumentationBestPractices.htm

https://redbooth.com/blog/main-roles-agile-team

https://www.cio.com/article/2432568/the-role-of-the-core-development-team-in-an-agile-project.html

https://www.cio.com/article/2432568/the-role-of-the-core-development-team-in-an-agile-project.html

https://medium.com/@agile42/introduction-to-agile-part-2-what-is-agile-f56103b9ad71

https://apiumhub.com/tech-blog-barcelona/building-agile-team/

https://www.scrum.org/resources/blog/about-self-organizing-teams

http://www.andycleff.com/2015/08/agile-best-practices-values-
principles-virtues/

https://medium.com/tech-travelstart/an-exercise-for-creating-a-team-
working-agreement-8672c0bf862c

https://www.atlassian.com/blog/agile/how-to-create-an-amazing-agile-
team

https://hbr.org/2016/05/embracing-agile

https://www.atlassian.com/agile/manifesto

https://techbeacon.com/app-dev-testing/agile-manifesto-dead

https://medium.com/@agile42/introduction-to-agile-part-1-why-are-
people-turning-to-agile-a542b70c01fb

Made in the USA
Coppell, TX
16 January 2020